MW01205273

It is an honor to write an endorsement for *Destiny*. This new book by Vas Yarosh is easily understood and will encourage readers to believe they have a destiny, to embrace that destiny, and even with failures and setbacks, to press toward that destiny. Great insights for everyone.

—Dr. Frank Damazio
President, Ministry Fellowship International

Destiny by Vas Yarosh is the most transformational book I have read in many years. Concise, to the point, and full of valuable tools for success, it is a must read for every person who seeks to reach their fullest potential as a human being. Vas speaks from the heart and with wisdom that grows out of his personal experience with God and in life. It is my hope that those who read this book will recognize that it is not just a one and done read but a personal manual to be referenced again and again for the valuable information that it contains. Putting into practice the eight steps unveiled in Destiny can change a life forever and bring one into the best life God intended for them. My hope is that Vas will continue to write and share the valuable insights God has blessed him with. Until then, keep this book close! Enjoy, grow, and live better!

—Brad Makowski, Lead Pastor, Anthem Church

Vas Yarosh has done a masterful job in reminding us that "we are God's workmanship created in Christ Jesus to do good deeds that He has prepared in advance for us to do." As you apply these principles and God's word to your life, I'm confident that you will discover and walk in your destiny.

—Doug Clay,
General Superintendent of the Assemblies of God, USA

I have had the wonderful opportunity to get to know Vas. I know deep down inside that he knows the Lord and has spent time in God's presence—from that has come this book. In Vas's well written book, he shares from his journey of walking with God and has provided key action steps towards what God has for each individual. Destiny is a great book to inspire and equip you to walk out your God-given destiny, as well as a book that can be used in a small group setting. My prayer for you as you read is that your spirit man would become ignited with faith to believe that God has a destiny for your life and He is going to help you as you take the steps of faith. God is raising up people in this hour who believe that their destiny is found in Christ and through Christ.

—Chris Overstreet,
Founder of Compassion To Action

VAS YAROSH

Destiny

8 STEPS TO A FULFILLED LIFE

Bright Books, 2019

Destiny: 8 Steps to a Fulfilled Life by Vas Yarosh ©2018 Vas Yarosh. Revised and expanded from a previous Russian language version published in Europe. All rights reserved.

Scripture quotations marked KJV are taken from the KING JAMES VERSION (KJV): KING JAMES VERSION, public domain.

Scripture quotations marked NKJV taken from the New King James Version®. Copyright © 1982 by Thomas Nelson. Used by permission. All rights reserved.

Scripture quotations marked NIV taken from the HOLY BIBLE, NEW INTERNA-TIONAL VERSION®. NIV®. Copyright © 1973, 1978, 1984 by International Bible Society. Used by permission of Zondervan. All rights reserved worldwide.

Scripture quotations marked NASB taken from the NEW AMERICAN STANDARD BIBLE®, Copyright ©1960, 1962, 1963, 1968, 1971, 1972, 1973, 1975, 1977, 1995 by The Lockman Foundation. Used by permission.

GOD'S WORD is a copyrighted work of God's Word to the Nations. Quotations are used by permission. Copyright 1995 by God's Word to the Nations. All rights reserved.

Scripture quotations marked ESV are from The ESV® Bible (The Holy Bible, English Standard Version®), copyright © 2001 by Crossway, a publishing ministry of Good News Publishers. Used by permission. All rights reserved.

Scriptures marked TPT are from The Passion Translation®. Copyright © 2017 by BroadStreet Publishing® Group, LLC. Used by permission. All rights reserved. thePassionTranslation.com

CONTENTS

STEP 6 – HABITS **145**

STEP 7 – CHARACTER **165**

STEP 8 – DESTINY **189**

DEDICATION

I dedicate this book to my family, students, and friends. I believe God blesses us all through our interaction with each other. He has sent many people into my life. Each has enriched it and proven to be a gift from Him. I also dedicate this work to you, the reader, and to all who are ready to grow into God's predetermined destiny.

GRATITUDE

A heartfelt THANK YOU to my God and Jesus for eternal salvation, mercy, and blessings in life! I am grateful to my amazing wife, Olya, for all her support and prayers. She is my friend and partner in ministry. I treasure her! I also thank my close friends and relatives who have contributed to the writing of this book. Thanks to New Beginnings Church—I am blessed to live and serve the Lord with all of you.

PREFACE

Every time I am in an airport, I pause to observe the activity around me. With passengers rushing in all directions, workers bustling through their tasks, and constant intercom announcements of arrivals and departures, the facility seems doomed to chaos. However, underneath all the apparent confusion lie the workings of a well-organized system.

In those moments, I like to think about the folks around me. Are they about to embark on a joyous journey or routine business? Perhaps they are returning filled with memories and not quite ready to rejoin the hum of working life. Is the first-time flier filled with anxiety or with anticipation?

Life is very much the same. We are all on a journey with a takeoff and arrival. We are not all going the same way at the same time. As with the passengers in the airport, we each make a conscious choice of which flight to take to arrive at a specific destination.

Unlike those customers who must commit to their chosen flight, God does offer us the opportunity to change our destination at any time in our journey because he never runs out of mercy.

Many of my students in Bible college pose the same questions: *What is God's will for my life? Do I have any real say in my life choices, or are they already predetermined by God? Is it possible to change my destiny?*

Many renowned persons in the Bible faced the same questions. Abraham, David, Esther—all faced a defining moment when they chose to embrace the destiny God laid out for them. Through setbacks and failures, they pressed on toward the calling they knew came from above.

Today, we also face challenges. Some are predetermined through our socioeconomic status or culture. Others arise from choices we make. Both affect our destiny.

The famous French sculptor, Auguste Rodin, demonstrated Michelangelo's principle of creating a masterpiece: Simply remove all unnecessary pieces from the block of marble. Let this book become a hammer in the hands of the Great Sculptor, our creator. Allow him to chip out all the surplus, unneeded bits from your life that could detract from the personal greatness he has determined for you.

It always thrills me to see my students yield to God's molding to achieve far more than they ever thought possible. Throughout history, great people have refused to allow physical or financial difficulties to rob them of all God planned for them. You can join this elite group because the list of God's heroes of faith is not yet complete.

Step up to the ticket counter of God's divine airport, and let's take off!

Step 1

Environment

ENVIRONMENT becomes Thoughts — Thoughts ⇢ Emotions — Emotions ⇢ Words
Words ⇢ Actions — Actions ⇢ Habits — Habits ⇢ Character
Character becomes your
DESTINY

The eyes reflect the soul.
The tongue reflects its society.
—Jules Renard

THE BIRTH OF GREATNESS

God, is my family cursed?

I sat in my favorite chair and pondered this question after returning from the funeral of an older brother. My family, immediate and some extended, had moved to the United States more than twenty years ago. I was the youngest of seven brothers and male cousins. Four of those had died between the ages of twenty and fifty. One suffered a severe accident. Another never married. Another had never fathered children. Some divorced. Others experienced violence and other challenging life situations.

Why, God? I prayed. *Why does our family endure so many tragedies when we all believe in you, we all attend church, we know the Bible? Are the males in my family cursed? Will I suffer the same fate? Is there no hope for me?*

"Daddy, I'm sorry you lost your brother."

"Yes, Daddy. I'm sorry, too." My children came into the living room to hug me, each attempting to give me some comfort. I looked up and saw the tender love and compassion in my wife's eyes over my grief. My phone pinged multiple times as *hundreds* of texts flowed through from my church family, all bearing words of comfort and hope.

I'm so blessed, God. I have family. I have so many people who love me and support me. How have I turned out so different from the rest of the boys in our family?

As I sat and pondered, I began tracing my own life and saw how God had led me on a different course. Understanding and praise erupted in my heart as I realized the specific steps he'd used to bring me to a much better destiny.

God has developed a specific plan for every one of his children, long before our birth. The Bible provides many wonderful examples of people who learned of and fulfilled that exact purpose.

Look at Jacob, for example. He got ahead by cheating his brother and uncle, until God met him alone and wrestled with him all night. A changed man, Jacob yielded in the morning and begged for a divine blessing. God granted his request, sealed it by changing his name from Jacob (supplanter) to Israel (prince), and through his sons formed the Twelve Tribes of Israel.

In another case, Esther obeyed her guardian's instructions once she learned her people faced annihilation. She realized God had placed her *inside* the king's palace to save the lives of all the Jews in the realm. And she did just that!

In a dramatic encounter with the Lord on the road to Damascus, Saul turned from his zeal for the capture of Christians to a new passion for spreading the gospel. As a result of this transformation, God changed his name from Saul (asked for God) to Paul (humble). Consequently, he became the most prolific writer of the New Testament.

So many others—Abraham, Daniel, David, even Jesus—followed a process to live out the purpose God the Father had planned for them.

Throughout history many others have discovered their own God-designed destiny. Martin Luther challenged the teachings of the Roman Catholic Church, thus spearheading the Reformation throughout continental Europe. Madame CJ Walker became the first female African-American millionaire with an innovative line of hair care products and Mary Kay Ash founded the incredibly successful Mary Kay Cosmetics. Michael Jordan failed to qualify for his high school's basketball team, but he worked hard, made it the following year, and went on to become one of greatest players of all time. Dr. Ben Carson left the ghetto to become one of the most renowned surgeons of our day. Billy Graham preached throughout the world and became a spiritual adviser to multiple national leaders. David Green (Hobby Lobby), Do Won Chang and Jin Sook Chang (Forever 21), Steve Jobs (Apple), evangelist David Wilkerson, Rick Warren, Henry Ford, and countless others followed a similar process, achieved their purpose, altered their particular environment, and experienced the satisfaction of fulfilling their divine calling.

After years of equipping others with what I'd learned, I came to realize that neither magic pills nor overnight success really exists. It takes hard work and perseverance in pursuing the common process that mobilizes us for his divine destiny.

I decided to write this book to share the eight steps God moved me through, which guaranteed a different outcome in my life from my male relations. Because of these steps, I continue to live a joy-filled life with my precious wife and children and lead a satisfying ministry. God walks with me step by step as I continue to pursue and accomplish all his plans for me.

You, too, were born for purpose. Your life is not random. Grab hold of the calling God has for *your* life. Don't wait around merely praying for something to happen. *Act* on it. Join the many others who are right now fulfilling their divine calling, changing history, and watching their dreams come true.

I based this book on the words spoken by Frank Outlaw, the late founder of the BI-LO grocery chain:

> Watch your thoughts, they become words;
> Watch your words, they become actions;
> Watch your actions, they become habits;
> Watch your habits, they become character;
> Watch your character, for it becomes your destiny.

However, I felt Outlaw left out two important elements: environment and emotions.

Environment shapes a person much the same as soil affects seeds. Just as each crop, be it oranges or cranberries, needs a specific environment that is most conducive to its needs, we as humans also need the right environment to ensure maximum productivity in our own lives. We thrive or struggle in direct connection to our surroundings.

Emotions also affect us. Uncontrolled anger will destroy us no matter how healthy our environment is. Thankfulness, however, produces joy even in difficult circumstances. Depression suppresses hope. Laughter pushes us through tough times.

For these reasons, I changed the saying to cover all eight elements required to achieve our destiny:

> Create your environment, it becomes your thoughts;
>
> Create your thoughts, they become your emotions;
>
> Create your emotions, they become your words;
>
> Create your words, they become your actions;
>
> Create your actions, they become your habits;
>
> Create your habits, they become your character;
>
> Create your character, it becomes your destiny.

Many Christians fail to answer God's full call on their lives, preferring the safety of mediocrity over pressing into the unknown. Often, they allow past hurts or failures to define them, instead of standing up again and pressing on toward their God-ordained goal (see Philippians 3:14).

Finding destiny takes commitment, focus, and endurance. God is calling you. Right now. Today. What is your answer?

God gave us all wings to fly. Let's study these eight steps together, starting with the environment that surrounds us. We'll learn to enjoy the journey together and move into our destiny!

SOCIAL ATMOSPHERE

*The atmosphere of life that we live in
is what forms the patterns of our thinking,
our priorities, and our values.*

Society pressures us into believing that if we use a certain personal care product, wear fashionable clothing, or buy a certain model of car, we will enjoy success—guaranteed. The reality is, we must each dig deep inside our beings to discover where our destiny begins and the necessary steps to accomplish it.

God created us as social beings. From birth, our personality develops through interpersonal relationships, first from our immediate and extended family. Later, we start making friends around the time we enter school. These relationships, along with our genetic makeup, life experience, and spiritual environment all work together, influencing our progress, and molding us into unique beings.

As important as genetics and physical surroundings are, the two factors that influence us the most are the social and spiritual environments in which we move. Do those around me value education and hard work? Or do they tell me getting by is enough? Does my church home allow the Holy Spirit to operate in freedom, or is it more interested in preserving tradition? Do other believers encourage me to pursue God's best in my life, or do they model mere shallow commitment?

A shocking example of how much physical and social environment affects us is the discovery of two feral children in India in 1920. A shepherd found the young girls, who had been living in the jungle among wolves for four years, and sought to rescue them. The older appeared to be about eight years old and the younger, perhaps four.

At the time of their discovery, both ate only raw meat, crawled around on hands and knees, and refused all attempts to clothe them. They howled at night and fought against personal hygiene. The younger died a year after her discovery. The older lived nine more years. By the time of her own death at age seventeen, she'd developed only to the level of a four-year-old child with a vocabulary of about forty-five words.[1]

Another example of extreme environmental influence is Vanya Yudin of Russia. His mother raised him with many birds and, although she fed him well, never engaged in any form of human communication. By the age of six, he expressed little emotion, chirped like a bird, and flapped his hands like wings.

In other cases of feral children such as these two examples, those who have sought to help them have found it extremely difficult to reintroduce them to human society and language. Their early environmental exposure left them too entrenched in its ways. Some recovered, others experienced only limited success. Much psychological research shows that people seldom rise above their social setting.

On the other hand, some do achieve great success when removed from a negative situation to one of loving encouragement. That's why the Bible teaches about resocializing (2 Corinthians 6:17). Michael Oher, featured in the movie *Blind Side*, was rescued from poverty by a Christian couple, Sean and Leigh Anne Tuohy. They provided him with a nurturing and accepting environment, helped him get caught up on his high school education, and treated him the same as their two biological children. Oher went on to graduate from Ole Miss (University of Mississippi) and has played professional football since 2009.

These and many other instances exist, each demonstrating the importance of environment and personal experience which shape our perception of the world throughout our entire lives.

FAMILY, FRIENDS AND ACQUAINTANCES

We become what we behold.
We shape our tools and then our tools shape us.
—Marshall McLuhan

Our family lays the foundation of our social development. In a healthy family environment we first learn who we are and what our world is like. We learn the basic principles of right and wrong. Our parents set behavioral boundaries and help to develop our self-esteem. They provide us with the preliminary understanding of love, care, protection, and respect. As we grow and develop our own personalities, however, our perspective of life and success sometimes conflicts with that of the very ones who nurtured us in the beginning.

Some families encourage their children with words of affirmation, such as *Good job* or *You can do whatever you set your mind to.* Others support their children by telling them, *Even if you don't succeed at your goal, we will continue to love and support you anyway.*

Some children are trained to be totally self-reliant and are told, *You must accomplish everything in life by yourself. Don't rely on anyone else. This is how we got where we are today; no one helped us, so don't expect any help from us. You need to fight your own battles and develop the willpower to meet your challenges.*

Still others hear only words of condemnation and derision: *You're good for nothing. A total loser. You'll never amount to anything.*

Such words, both positive and negative, shape children's perceptions of themselves because they instinctively believe whatever their parents tell them. Consequently, they learn how to risk, persevere, and overcome difficulties to achieve success or go on to prove their parents' negative words correct by failing at anything they attempt. Others, determined to prove their parents wrong, go on to achieve success on their own, fueled with that desire within them.

My family supported me very little as I matured. They felt education was useless in the real world and all I needed was a basic skill set to survive—not thrive. Why? Were they cruel and unfeeling?

No! They advised me from their own personal experience of growing up in the Ukraine, where they faced, at that time, famine and persecution. Consequently, they believed that basic manual labor skills would provide more security and protect me against any lack in the future, rather than gambling everything on an education that provided no security against the unknown.

I cried out to God because I felt I needed something different. Something more. He answered my prayers by planting the desire for a higher education deep in my spirit. God knew he had to remove me from the environment of my childhood and place me in a totally different one to change my destiny.

I moved to a different city to attend college. It was the change God knew I needed. He placed people in my life who challenged and encouraged me to expand my knowledge. This molded me into a different person and thus propelled me forward to my purpose for my life.

The opinions of others continue to influence us all through life. Sometimes we fall into the trap of focusing on their perceptions of us to the point of adhering to those views. We allow those opinions to mold our self-value and eventually make ourselves hostage to those misconceptions, always trying—and usually failing—to please those people rather than focus on what our Maker sees in us.

Examine the voices you are listening to. Do they build you up or tear you down? Do they push you toward or tear you away from your destiny? Listen to those who affirm your value as God's own created one, born to succeed in his purpose.

The people around us—friends, family, coworkers, those who circulate in our social environment—all affect our daily life. According to Psalm 1, written by King David, the surest way for success and happiness is for the individual to be in the *right place* among the *right people* and to perceive life through the lens of *God's given destiny*.

Show me your friends and I'll tell you who you are[2] is a popular saying which aptly characterizes us in our surroundings. For, in the same way seawater shapes stones, our friends and family influence us. Relationships are never neutral. They either drive us forward and upward, or drag us down and backward.

Think about that!

Every friendship influences us and plays a role in our lives. Harboring a relationship that does nothing to enrich our spirit and soul most likely robs us. True friendships help us toward balance, wholeness, and maturity. False friendships drain us.

That second group of friends is happy to consume all our time, attention, strength, and emotions, which can eventually affect our mental, emotional, spiritual, and physical health. Perhaps this is why Paul wrote a severe warning: "Bad company corrupts good character" (1 Corinthians 15:33).

Look at King Rehoboam, son of King Solomon. He ignored the wisdom of his elders and chose to consult with his own young, arrogant, ambitious, and egocentric friends (1 Kings 12). That decision caused the kingdom to split into two, which further resulted in much bloodshed between the two kingdoms for many years.

Two of David's sons came to tragic ends for listening to corrupt advice. Amnon, after lusting for his half-sister, listened to his cousin and raped her through deception. Absalom later set an ambush and had him murdered.

When Absalom began lusting after the throne, Ahithophel, a trusted counselor for David, forsook the king and encouraged Absalom to overthrow his father. Absalom's arrogance against his father, his king, and his God cost him his life.

Whom do you turn to for counsel? Supportive friendships neither drain nor destroy, but they *do* point you toward the truth. Do you prefer to listen to those who will tell you what you want to hear or to people who will give you truth, no matter how painful? Again, evaluate your friendships. Does each build you up and make you a better person? Does this person help you toward the destiny God has planned for your life? Do you need to let some friendships die to move toward that destiny?

> Entrepreneurs know the value of healthy connections to guarantee success and cultivate them with great care and strategy.

As in the business sector, entrepreneurs know the value of healthy connections to guarantee success and cultivate them with great care and strategy. The same is true with good friendships. They take time to develop but provide an invaluable investment toward future success as a mature and contented believer in Jesus.

God has invested in you. Heavily. He prepared unlimited resources for us and gave us access to them. It's time for you to invest in yourself. This is accomplished through the next section—our spiritual environment.

1-Duy Pham, Unsplash

THE ATMOSPHERE
OF HEAVEN

The more densely God's atmosphere
dwells in your home and church,
the more complete his plan of your destiny.

David knew how God delights in changing people's destiny. God took him from one of the lowliest jobs in the land, tending sheep, to shepherding the entire country as king. God used what he learned living with the sheep to run the nation.

Can you imagine yourself working as a janitor in Walmart to becoming the CEO of a major corporation? Why not? Can God not change your own life as drastically as David's?

Consider Psalm 1 again, where David highlights the habits that bring the fruit of success:

> Blessed is the one who does not walk in step with the wicked or stand in the way that sinners take
> or sit in the company of mockers,
> but whose delight is in the law of the LORD,
> and who meditates on his law day and night.
> That person is like a tree planted by streams of water, which yields its fruit in season and whose leaf does not wither— whatever they do prospers. (verses 1-3 NIV)

What are those streams of water David wrote about? Where did he plant himself? In God's presence. Alone in the field, David discovered the unseen, spiritual atmosphere of heaven, where he spent time with God. He learned how to enter into that dimension, which became as real to him as his physical environment. From those times, he drew strength, vision, and wisdom.

David recognized how those streams produced fruit in his spirit and brought prosperity into his life. Although his brothers lived in the same house

We create the spiritual atmosphere we dwell in through our intimacy with God.

and experienced the same Jewish rituals, they failed to tap into the beauty and reality of God's presence.

The same is true today. Two people can exist in the same house, surrounded by the same family, and attend the same church. One keeps his spirit close to the refreshing water of God's presence, while the other exists in a spiritual desert. *We* create the spiritual atmosphere we dwell in through our intimacy with God.

This principle exists among churches as well. Some cling to old traditions as a means to salvation, only to become dry and parched. Others flow with the life-giving water Jesus offers by giving the Holy Spirit total freedom to move throughout the congregation. The worshipers find themselves spiritually satisfied and growing stronger in their spiritual walk every day.

Genesis 1:2 describes the Holy Spirit hovering over the water, as though he provided the atmosphere through which the physical world was created. When God appeared to Old Testament people, he surrounded them with that extraordinary presence. It transformed those individuals. God's presence *is* the atmosphere of heaven. This unseen dimension is true reality.

Consider how the Holy Spirit infused Gideon with courage (Judges 6 & 7). He found Gideon hiding in terror, took him from that place, and transformed him into a faith-filled warrior who conquered the same enemy he had feared—with a mere 300 soldiers.

In Ezekiel 37, the Holy Spirit moved once again when he showed the prophet a mighty vision of a valley of countless dry bones. He asked Ezekiel to prophesy the impossible. When Ezekiel obeyed God, he was transformed from a man filled with words of woe and doom to one who proclaimed hope and optimism.

After the resurrection and ascension of Jesus, the Holy Spirit came as promised (Acts 2), empowering the 120 faithful followers of Jesus (aka the former deserters who had scattered at the time of Jesus's death) to be daring declarers of the *good news*. He also changed Saul, a murderer of God's people, to the most dynamic and passionate disciple of them all.

What an atmosphere! The atmosphere of heaven. *This* is true reality, powerful enough to transform each of us into a new dimension of being: Christ *in* us. This mystery, hidden for generations, is now revealed to you and me, "Christ in you, the hope of glory" (Colossians 1:26–27). Even today, some read those verses, even memorize them, but fail to grasp the full impact. Those who have received the spiritual knowledge of it live changed and fulfilled lives.

Today, this spiritual environment resides anywhere: in a Holy Spirit-filled body of believers, in our homes, in our very hearts. Peter and Paul lived in this reality as they boldly proclaimed the power of the gospel. They understood the power of resurrection and lived it.

Peter and Paul each enjoyed an intimate relationship with God as Father, Son, and Holy Spirit, receiving special knowledge, revelation, and spiritual strength to serve the people, and they suffered—with joy—for that service. They so saturated themselves in this divine atmosphere that they became *carriers* of it. Peter's very shadow healed the sick. Paul sang praises in prison with a bruised and bloodied body. Heaven came down to that prison, burst the gates wide open, and caused the salvation of everyone present. Such is the power of heaven's atmosphere. The longer a person dwells in that atmosphere, the stronger and more mature he or she becomes.

Although God exists everywhere, he manifests himself differently in some places. Sometimes God manifests himself so powerfully that people can no longer stand on their feet as their physical bodies meet his presence. He may supernaturally heal a broken body or spirit as people pray. Or, he will so fill a person with his presence that they can endure suffering with great joy.

The most memorable moments of my life are those when I have experienced that spiritual dimension. How I love to dwell in such a glorious state of being. Life is worth living if only to experience that!

The key to the throne room of God's glory is prayer and meditation. Some people struggle to understand the importance of prayer. Others understand that prayer transports us to a different dimension, a dimension ruled by different laws.

God's realm has no time—not as we understand time. Time, he created for our three-dimensional world, but the spirit realm exists outside it.

I remember the first time I stepped into God's dimension. I enjoyed his presence so much that later, when I looked at my clock, I thought it was broken, because a few hours had passed by! Surely I'd prayed for only a few minutes. That experience changed me forever. I longed to go deeper and deeper in my relationship with God.

Such times are so profound they leave an imprint on our soul and alter our destiny. The unseen world is real and eternal. What we see with our natural eyes is only temporary. Everything temporary (including time) flees in the face of the eternal.

Each time I pray, I *expect* to encounter the beauty, tranquility, and joy of the spiritual world. The longer I pray, the more saturated I become with God's endless love and peace. It cannot be explained or understood by the human mind because it comes from a place far beyond human comprehension.

Even the Apostle Paul stated as much when he wrote, "The peace of God, which surpasses all understanding, will guard your hearts and your minds through Christ Jesus" (Philippians 4:7 ESV). God's peace comes to us through proactive faith and is received only by encountering him through his word and in prayer. The whole person is renewed in these precious moments of dwelling in God's presence.

Not only does the Holy Spirit renew our hearts and mind, he also re-charges every cell of our body. That is why spiritual nourishment and the spiritual atmosphere in which we *dwell* are the most important elements of heaven's environment for our life. These shape our destiny. The more we focus on them, the more influence they have on the other steps that lead us to that end.

THE HOLY OF HOLIES

In the Old Testament, God brought his presence to earth in the holy of ho-lies, the most sacred place of the tabernacle. He instructed Moses to build the movable structure during their forty-year journey to the Promised Land. The tabernacle consisted of three sections: the outer court, the holy place and the most holy place, or holy of holies.

Only one priest entered this last area, and only once a year. First, he had to sacrifice an animal in the outer court. After entering the holy place, he washed his hands and feet at the golden laver and offered incense, which symbolized the people's prayers, on another altar. Only then could he proceed to the holy of holies where God's presence met with him at the ark of the covenant. It held three items: the stone tablets on which were written the Ten Commandments; a pot of manna, the heavenly food that sustained Israel for their forty years in the desert; and Aaron's rod, which had supernatural powers. Two cherubim crowned the lid of the ark. This lid symbolized God's throne, and from that place, God spoke to men. Moses modeled the tabernacle on the heavenly tabernacle God had shown him in a vision. The writer of Hebrews mentions this several times.

In the heavenly tabernacle, Jesus is the high priest, and through his authority, each of us is granted access to the holy of holies. In this place, God desires to meet with his human creation at a deep and intimate level. It's from here that our true purpose unfolds.

God created humanity in his image, which is comprised of three parts: body, soul, and spirit. Our body provides contact with the physical world. This is like the outer court of the tabernacle. The soul, which consists of the mind, feelings, and will, is like the holy place where the bread of the presence, the lampstand, and altar of incense stood.

The spirit in us allows us to connect with the spiritual world. Only in the spirit can we experience the holy of holies to commune with God. Before we can step into that sacred place, we must first stop in the outer court to offer our bodies to him as a "living sacrifice" (Romans 12:1) of total dedication and devotion.

We nourish our souls in the holy place by feeding on the heavenly bread, which is the Word of God. The lamp symbolizes the work of the Holy Spirit. He sheds light on our innermost thoughts and desires as we interact with him, giving us the opportunity to repent and cleanse our hearts and desires. The seven branches of the lamp represent the fullness and perfection of God's grace in our lives.

The Holy Spirit next takes us to the altar of incense, which stood at the entrance to the holy of holies. Only in spirit can we meet and communicate with him. Here is where we receive the Word (Ten Commandments) and supernatural provision (the manna). Afterward, everything that was dried up in our life begins to blossom (as did Aaron's rod).

In prayer, we must allow ourselves to be filled with the Holy Spirit, claim the blood of Jesus Christ on our lives, and in the spirit come into God's presence. Once we've arrived in this place, our spirit, soul, and body relax to the point that we cease to exist in human time. Our spirit connects us to God's sphere, which exists outside of time. As we immerse ourselves in this heavenly atmosphere, it saturates us until, like Peter and Paul, we become carriers of it. We're charged with peace and faith. As we carry this presence with us, it permeates our homes and family. This unseen energy brings life to all that is visible around us.

> The more we experience God's presence in church, at home, and in the workplace, the more completely his perfect plan is accomplished in our lives.

Our spouses and children also blossom in that environment, where they can develop their own sense of destiny and experience more contentment. Thus, the potential of every family member is unlocked when we carry the atmosphere we've received from time spent in the holy of holies into our homes. Our other earthly relationships improve as well because God has spoken to us, guided us, and inspired us to new horizons. The more we experience God's presence in church, at home, and in the workplace, the more completely his perfect plan is accomplished in our lives.

These moments of dwelling in God's realm will continue shaping our lives. They form our beliefs, ignite our faith, shape our emotions, and influence the words we speak.

How we master the first step, Environment, will impact the next, Thinking. Let's not halt along the way. Keep moving forward, intentionally creating a spiritual environment inside of us and the social group around us. We can let circumstances rule us, or we can take control and rule our lives from within. We want to press on—blossoming, growing, and reaching out—just like Aaron's rod.

HALFWAY FAITH

It is easier to lead people
than to get them moving.
—David Fank

The Lord decided to bless Abram and to change his destiny. God had said to him, "Go from your country, your people and your father's household to the land I will show you. I will make you into a great nation, and I will bless you; I will make your name great, and you will be a blessing" (Genesis 12:1–2 NIV). Why did God tell Abram to leave his home and country? Could he bless him in his place? Could he give Abram's great destiny as Abraham right there, surrounded by familiar surroundings, acquaintances, and friends? No! God needed to remove him from the harmful and deceptive influence of worshiping false gods and into a *new environment*, one surrounded by God's own divine presence and purpose: the founding of a great nation.

God will challenge every follower to leave his or her comfort area behind and press on. What holds *you* back? Is it your mindset, lifestyle, friends, or misplaced priorities? Are you ready to leave anyone or anything necessary to press forward to God's highest call on your life?

Notice that Terah, Abram's father, received the initial revelation of the Promised Land (Genesis 11:31). After gathering up his family, he left Ur of the Chaldeans and headed for the place of God's choosing. But after entering the city of Haran, he settled down and stayed.

Terah started out well, taking his entire family out of Ur, but he never left Haran. Perhaps he liked

" Refuse to imprison your soul within the confines of religious rites and the opinions of society. **"**

the city and got attached to it. Or, its name reminded him of his own son, Haran, who had died. Maybe a deep depression or grief from his great loss prevented him from pursuing God's promise to the end. Or, he could have simply settled for a life of mediocrity over the challenge of the unknown.

In any case, he never fulfilled God's full purpose for him and his family. After Terah's death, Abram remembered God's promise and set out to fulfill his complete destiny. In my years of ministry, I've seen so many believers who end up in the same manner—stuck somewhere between what they left and where they were meant to go. Because of that, they never achieve their full potential in God.

After leaving my childhood home for the university, I moved again, leaving behind a good job and new friends to pursue the destiny God had revealed to me. Often I moved from one step to the next with little understanding, but trusting him for my future. Those two moves impacted my view of life, developed my character, and brought about the fulfillment of my calling.

> ʕʕ Our world in which we live and work is a mirror of our faith, enthusiasm, and expectations. ʔʔ

Every person will face this sort of struggle. Once we've received a revelation from God, will we follow him into the fearful unknown or remain in the comfort of the familiar? Don't live life halfway between the two. Leave behind the bondage of sin, generational mindsets, dead religion, and anything else that holds you back from becoming all God intended you to be.

Refuse to imprison your soul within the confines of religious rites and the opinions of society. Stay firm. Like Abraham, count the grains of sand under your feet, gaze at the myriads of stars over your head, and remember God's personal promises to you. *Remember,* and keep moving.

Never give up on the place God has prepared for you. God will show you, just as He showed Joshua what he needed to succeed. *"Keep this Book of the Law always on your lips; meditate on it day and night, so that you may be careful to do everything written in it. Then you will be prosperous and successful" (Joshua 1:8 NIV).*

As you saturate yourself in God's presence, your family will feel the effects. Our world in which we live and work is a mirror of our faith, enthusiasm, and expectations. God longs to give you and your family his very best. Learn to bless your family. Cherish your spouse and affirm your children.

Bless those around you. Bring the atmosphere of heaven into your home, neighborhood, job, and church as you fulfill the words of Jesus: "Let your kingdom come ... your will be done ... on earth as it is done in heaven."

AIR OF LIFE

*Our climate depends
on the people that surround us.*
—Mark Twain

I grew up in a heavily industrialized area in the Ukraine. Multiple smokestacks belched out smog, and every inhabitant had to breathe this air. While nobody has died immediately from this pollution, the constant intake has caused many chronic health issues.

Our bodies and brains need clean oxygen for peak function. Medical researchers put tomato plants in a special greenhouse, infused with extra oxygen. They discovered the plants grew taller and bore extra fruit. When they applied oxygen to patients' wounds, they healed faster.

Doctors have found that after spending time in an oxygen chamber, people have been healed of many illnesses, including arthritis, multiple sclerosis, liver diseases, blindness, deafness, leprosy, diabetic gangrene, and many more.

2-Daniel Spase, Unsplash

My question to you is this: What air do you breathe? The pollution of anger, hate, discontent, greed? Or do you inhale God's pure oxygen of love, peace, and joy? Are our homes polluted with discouraging or demeaning words which bring death? Or do we inspire our loved ones with affirming and accepting words?

YOU HEAR AND SEE WHAT?

ChildWise, an English research agency, published a report after surveying two thousand children from the ages of five to sixteen. They concluded that individuals spend much more time on electronic devices than interacting with persons in the same household. They reported that mothers spend an average of forty to sixty minutes a day interacting with their children, while fathers spend a mere five minutes.[3]

Dr. Emma Bond, University of Suffolk, an expert on individuals and modern technology in society, believes that mobile devices have become "virtual babysitters," replacing much of hands-on parenting.[4]

Kaiser Family Foundation maintains that American children and teens spend almost eight hours on electronic devices every day, surfing the web or playing video games.[5] Many electronic games involve violence. The child plays the game and sees the hero or villain dying and brought back to life for the next game play, completely obscuring the reality and finality of death and obliterating the sanctity of life.

Many movies, games, and even cartoons involve violence. Others introduce children to witchcraft through the appeal of the world of magic.

Another powerful agent of influence in our air is listening to music. Some heavy metal music, rap songs, and other genres exalt violence, hatred of authority, and demeaning of women.

I read an article about a teenager who killed his parents and a sibling. Immediately afterwards, he began playing a song that spewed out hateful words, including the words, *I want you dead.* Allegedly, he kicked the bodies of his dead parents to the beat of the music.[6]

For my readers raising children, take heed. The constant messages of such music will affect your child. Make no mistake. All types of media, while essentially good, can be detrimental to your children if they go unchecked. No human is strong enough to withstand the filth, hatred, and put-downs of TV, movies, games, or music. Protect the children in your care. Protect their spiritual air as you would protect them from a physical pollution. Raise them with healthy, wholesome music, games, and quality time. God has entrusted them to you to raise properly.

THE KEY

God showed Joshua what he needed to succeed in life. "Keep this Book of the Law always on your lips; meditate on it day and night, so that you may be careful to do everything written in it. Then you will be prosperous and successful" (Joshua 1:8 NIV). As a parent, it is your responsibility to set the air of the home for your children by getting and keeping them immersed in God's Word, in prayer, and in being around like-minded people. As you saturate yourself in God's presence, your children will observe and be affected. God wants only the best for you, your spouse, and your family. He can be trusted.

Learn to bless your family. Affirm your children. Bless those around you. Teach your children how to give from the heart. One of the greatest gifts, which costs nothing, is a smile. Smile at your spouse, your children, your friends, strangers. By doing so, you will be spreading God's love and peace.

TALE OF TWO FAMILIES

I don't know who my grandfather was;
I am much more concerned
to know what his grandson will be.
—Abraham Lincoln

Between 1868 and 1874, a sociologist and prison inspector, Richard L. Dugdale, toured thirteen facilities in New York. After finding numerous inmates related to one another, he conducted a separate study to discover if environment had contributed heavily to their lives of crime. He purported that the patriarch of this particular clan had lived a godless life and raised his children the same. He further alleged that of more than one thousand descendants studied, three hundred died prematurely, one hundred spent an average of thirty years in prison, almost two hundred turned to prostitution, and at least one hundred became alcoholics.

After Dugdale published his findings in 1877, the story so intrigued a minister that he decided to study the life of Jonathan Edwards, a well-known preacher who was born around the same time and lived in the same state as the prison inspector's subject. Credited with starting the Great Awakening of his time, Jonathan Edwards's descendants include three U.S. Senators, three governors, sixty-five professors, 100 lawyers, three mayors, thirteen college presidents, thirty judges, 100 missionaries, sixty authors, and a vice-president of the United States.[7]

According to George Whitefield, another powerful preacher who participated in the Great Awakening, he found great peace and harmony in the Edwards home. He found the children respectful and the parents quite loving toward one another and all their children. This home life so impressed Whitefield that he sought to find a wife as good as Mrs. Edwards.

> **Harmony dwells in homes where the Word of God is honored and read regularly.**

Experience has proven countless times that harmony dwells in homes where the Word of God is honored and read regularly. Families who worship and pray together enjoy God's peace, joy, and love. This nurturing environment helps develop the family unity as well as each individual. It helps them to behave in positive ways toward one another and grow in faith. They display courage during difficult times and encourage one another through them. All this is maintained through constant forgiveness and mercy (Matthew 6:14–15).

Jonathan Edwards left behind a good name, which is mentioned in Ecclesiastes 7:1. In God's eyes, that good name is far more important than material wealth. Striving to leave this legacy ensures that we will maintain high moral values that honor God and bless those around us.

Besides family, our choice of friends greatly influences us on this journey. King Solomon stated, "As iron sharpens iron, so a man sharpens the countenance of his friend" (Proverbs 27:17 NLT). We influence our friends and they influence us. This truth cannot be denied. Take a moment to ask yourself if you are creating an atmosphere of love and trust in your family, among your friends and coworkers—or the *opposite*.

My prayer is that this book becomes a catalyst for you. May God help you to change, to rewrite your personal stories, and take hold of his call on your life. I invite you to not only read the book, but also to uncover the buried treasure hidden in the hearts of every one of you. May you experience a true God encounter as you read and meditate to help you to set achievable goals. Join me in this prayer:

> *Heavenly Father, as your children, we want to see and understand you more through the reading of this book. Let your kingdom come, and firmly establish it in our hearts. Give us your power and knowledge to know how to apply what we learn in our everyday lives. Give us the ability to live and speak your plans and destiny for ourselves and our families. Help us to build the right spiritual atmosphere in our hearts, families, and workplaces. Surround us with people who will work with us to advance your kingdom on earth and enjoy the process. We acknowledge that you hold our future in your hands. Give us grace to establish your kingdom in our lives. In Jesus's name we pray. Amen.*

QUESTIONS FOR REFLECTION:

1. Evaluate the atmosphere in your own home, your family, friends, and coworkers.

2. What can you do to change the atmosphere?

3. Who are your friends? Who influences you, and whom do you influence?

Thoughts

Environment becomes **THOUGHTS** — Thoughts --→ Emotions — Emotions --→ Words

Words --→ Actions — Actions --→ Habits — Habits --→ Character

Character becomes your

DESTINY

You become what you think about.
—Earl Nightingale

I once heard a story of a man who visited Hawaii. While there, he saw a beautiful home situated on a mountain. It overlooked all the lovely beaches below. As he admired the building's location, he thought to himself, *I can't even imagine myself living in such a wonderful place.*

A second thought swiftly followed.

Don't worry, because you're right. It'll never happen.

That startled him. Frightened him.

"God, is that you?" he whispered. He paused. "What is it that you're trying to tell me?"

If you can't imagine something, it will never happen.

Thoughts define our future.

Our physical and spiritual environments influence how we think. However, the process of thought alone is powerful and creative. Once we fully understand the message of this chapter and apply it to our lives, we will never be the same!

THOUGHTS ARE TANGIBLE

Every thought we think
is creating our future.
—Louise L. Hay

What are thoughts? Can we measure or weigh them? After pondering the process of thought, I've come to the conclusion that they are not just invisible energy; they are tangible. Everything we see, touch, build, and cultivate is material and tangible, yet was birthed through *thought*. Therefore, I maintain that thoughts are the thickest form of spirit or thinnest part of matter. Even scientists confirm the material nature of thoughts. They agree that thoughts transcend our familiar five senses of taste, touch, smell, hearing, and sight.

> ❝ Thoughts are the thickest form of spirit or thinnest part of matter. ❞

Every object has density. Wood, stone, and iron have higher chemical compositions than water or soil, but all are visible matter. There is also matter we don't see, yet experience. We can't see wind, but nobody argues its reality. We don't taste fresh air, but we appreciate its refreshing purity.

The same is true of thoughts. They influence not only us as individuals but also those around us like magnets that attract certain metals and draw them close. Both thought and magnetic force remain unseen, but have visible results. A dog cowers from its owner's angry thoughts punctuated by words. A child pauses at the side of a busy road at the mother's cry of warning.

God *thought* creation before speaking it out. Ben Carson *thought* of being a doctor and found ways to turn that into reality. Michael Jordan *thought* of being a great basketball player and practiced countless hours to succeed. Michelangelo *thought* the statue of David before he chiseled the concept from the marble.

Thoughts produce action. We think before we cook, balance our checkbooks, or drive a car. Thoughts remain unseen but not their manifestations. Creative ideas put into motion have become amazing artistic works, such as Queen Elizabeth Park in Vancouver, B.C., and the world-renowned Empire State Building in New York City.

On a smaller scale, one may drive through any neighborhood and notice the creativity of some homeowners, whose *thoughts* have developed a lovely, tranquil landscape. Thousands of thoughts pass through our minds every day, from fleeting to serious. Deciding what to wear, what to eat for breakfast, and whether to chance running that yellow light are thoughts that buzz through our brain, are contemplated, then acted on or discarded in mere moments. Serious thoughts, such as educational choices, job changes, and whom to marry, remain for longer periods.

3-Pietro Tebaldi, Unsplash

MIND AND HEART THOUGHTS

Great thoughts come from the heart.

— Luc de Clapiers

Why do positive thinking, declarations, and confessions of faith fail to work for some people? We need to look into the inner being for the answer. Every thought is like a rock thrown into a calm lake. It quickly sinks to the bottom, but the ripples it leaves behind tell us of its location. Small rocks leave small ripples. Larger ones make waves.

Such is the strength of thoughts. We must know the origin. A quick, fleeting thought, like what to eat for breakfast or our clothing choice for the day, ripples through our mind and is quickly gone.

A strong thought, however, such as a revelation from God, impacts our spirit being in a huge and lasting way. It becomes part of us and influences our entire life. Those thoughts become our beliefs and change the outlook of our life.

Fleeting thoughts have the power to generate fleeting emotions. These emotions exist only as long as we are focused on a certain thought. Beliefs work at a much deeper, perhaps even subconscious, level. For this reason, attempting to practice positive thinking fails to work for some. True life change requires deep conviction.

Beliefs and convictions are dominant in our thinking. Such thoughts appear without any effort and control our lives. Our subconscious minds are the thoughts of the heart. Shallow, short-lived thoughts change our emotions for a very short time, but convictions lead to long-term feelings. If one believes child abuse is wrong, the thought of it evokes strong emotion. Those feelings reflect our true self. It is not a flash of anger from being cut off in traffic, but rather a burning in the soul that challenges us to rise up and take action.

We do not determine our future by what we hope to become, but rather by who we already *are*. Most of our success is defined by the actions that come out of our inner man. One understands many things through thoughts in the mind, but convictions from the heart work to shape our destiny.

> ❝ We do not determine our future by what we hope to become, but rather by who we already are. ❞

Thoughts are not convictions; nevertheless, convictions develop from intense or repeated thoughts. Convictions run deeper than thoughts. They lay hidden in our hearts and affect our perception of the world. An abused woman may conclude that all men are batterers; a child living in an abusive environment may become certain that lying is the only way to survive.

On the other hand, if children grew up with parents who maintained strong ties to God, they may have developed the deep conviction that serving God with one's whole heart is worth the cost, no matter how much goes wrong in life. Through the environment their parents created, the children also tasted God's faithful presence in any challenging situation.

To illustrate further, look at the convictions of Mother Teresa in helping the destitute people of India. She embraced abject poverty, yet her whole being radiated the love and peace of God. When given a car, she sold it and used the money to start a leper colony. Her deep convictions kept her life on course, doing what she felt God had called her to do.

Conviction works like that because it is rooted deep within us, affecting our every thought and action. It is that deep-seated belief in oneself that drives an Olympic hopeful to maintain a strict diet, even when surrounded by sugary treats, because the desire for the goal supersedes the craving for immediate gratification.

Your coworkers may attempt to goad you into doctoring reports or indulging in personal fun on company time, yet conviction reminds you that it is the same as stealing. In this case, conviction is your subconscious thoughts, which are planted deep in your heart and therefore overrule any short-term conflicts that challenge your integrity.

For these reasons, positive thinking on its own cannot work. Unless such "positive" thoughts anchor on conviction, any change is simply temporary. I cannot fake how I feel about myself unless I know and believe what God thinks about me. Unless I cling to the truth of Psalm 139:14 (*GOD'S WORD*)—"I will give thanks to you because I have been so amazingly and miraculously made. Your works are miraculous, and my soul is fully aware of this"—I can tell myself hundreds of times that I'm worthy, but unless I believe that fact in my heart, the words remain useless.

The Bible says to "Train up a child in the way he should go, and even when he is old he will not turn away from it" (Proverbs 22:6 *GOD'S WORD*). Many parents who have raised their children with God's principles have seen them stray as adults. Despite that show of rebellion, some do come back to the convictions instilled in them as children. Franklin

> " True creativity, wisdom, and inspiration develop in the heart, not in the mind. "

Graham is such an example. Growing up under the shadow of his famous father, Billy Graham, he rebelled by taking to drinking and partying. Then, at twenty-two, he came face to face with Jesus in Jerusalem, returned to the training of his childhood, and now heads up his own worldwide ministry, Samaritan's Purse.

As I wrote before, those profound beliefs become part of our deepest being. They override those temporary thoughts that flit through our minds—which only have the power to inspire us temporarily and do not impact our future. True creativity, wisdom, and inspiration develop in the heart, not in the mind.

Thoughts can describe our intentions or who we wish to be. Conviction—*heart* thoughts—describe who we truly *are*.

REPROGRAMMING YOUR THERMOSTAT

Think in the morning. Act in the noon.
Eat in the evening. Sleep in the night.
—William Blake

I love fresh air, even in the wintertime. After opening several windows to allow it to flow through the house, the interior temperature drops. I close all the windows and allow the thermostat to "talk to" the furnace, and soon our home is as toasty warm as we desire.

That's the beauty of thermostats in our modern era. We set the thermostat to a certain temperature, and winter or summer, this wonderful gadget keeps our dwellings at the predetermined level we set with the push of a button.

Conviction works like an inner thermostat in our hearts. A person can soar above their convictions for a short time or descend lower but will always come back to the constant of the heart's convictions. When we wander, through laziness or temptation, the thermostat signals the furnace, our conscience, which activates our core beliefs to bring us back to the "preset temperature" of life choices that honor God and keep us moving forward toward success.

Our deepest thoughts define who we really are. They work much like a programmed computer. Should a virus invade, everything mutates and shuts down. The virus may be unforgiveness or offense, worry, fear, or envy. If we neglect to remove the virus, even our body suffers through illness, broken relationships, or stress.

4- Nest

The only way to fulfill your God-intended destiny is to change your core convictions. Like reprogramming your home thermostat to a desired temperature, you must adjust how you think. The old, entrenched thought patterns that have failed you many times cannot solve any of life's problems. Only by forming new thought patterns will you experience victory in the mind.

> " The only way to fulfill your God intended destiny is to change your core convictions. "

Many of our thought processes came to us through generations that preceded us. Scientists have concluded that each cell in our body is like a computer. Not only does it contain our own unique information but also what we've inherited from prior generations, which in turn, influences our life experience and belief systems.

For example, if a person believes that God works only in a specific way, he limits God's ability to work in any other way for his own life. If he expects to endure great difficulty in life, hardship comes. Like a magnet, he draws that expectation to him, thus making it a reality. Another person may believe that blessing only comes to those who deserve it. Her own faulty thermostat deems her unworthy. Consequently, she fails to receive all God has planned for her.

This book is all about reprogramming the mind, the heart. If you believe, like Paul, that you can do anything through Christ's strength, you will (Philippians 4:13).

Often, people ask me, "What should I do with my life?"

I generally tell them, "It doesn't matter what you *do*. Nothing will change until you understand who you *are*. You must change any negative images you hold of yourself in your heart. Your destiny will never change until you change and transform your subconscious thoughts."

Paul calls this the "renewing of the mind" (Romans 12:2). This means we must return to humanity's original state *before* the fall. Renewing—restarting—our thought process is difficult because we must *rethink* how we think. Only a completely renewed mind comprehends God's will, which changes how we view ourselves and our own abilities. Two main factors always involved in reprogramming the heart are *information* and *emotion*. We cannot change anything for good outside of us without first influencing our heart. When we understand our identity in God and view reality from his perspective, our perception of ourselves changes. This empowers us to press on to the destiny of his choosing.

The Bible shows how God pays attention to our hearts more than our deeds, shown by the following verses:

> "Let the words of my mouth and the meditation of my heart be acceptable in your sight, O Lord, my strength and my redeemer" (Psalm 19:14 KJV).

> "As for you, my son Solomon, know the God of your father, and serve him with a loyal heart and with a willing mind; for the Lord searches all hearts and understands all the intent of the thoughts. If you seek him, he will be found by you; but if you forsake him, he will cast you off forever" (1 Chronicles 28:9 NKJV).

"But the Lord said to Samuel, "Do not look at his appearance or at his physical stature, because I have refused him. For the Lord does not see as man sees; for man looks at the outward appearance, but the Lord looks at the heart" (1 Samuel 16:7 NKJV).

Solomon warned his readers, "As a man thinketh in his heart, so is he" (Proverbs 23:7 KJV). Just as Michelangelo, from the picture in his head, chipped David from marble, so our thoughts shape who and what we become. Positive thoughts create life and success. Negative ones choke and kill.

Paul agreed with this concept in Romans 8:5–6 (NKJV): "For those who live according to the flesh set their minds on the things of the flesh, but those who live according to the Spirit, the things of the Spirit. For the carnally minded is death, but to be spiritually minded is life and peace."

Paul is showing two vastly different mindsets and their end results. Carnal thoughts lead to a shallow existence that ends in spiritual death. Guiding our thoughts to spiritual principles and values leads to peace, fulfillment, and a productive spiritual life. Mind transformation happens when we gaze on God's glory. As we focus on him—*his* power, *his* beauty, *his* love—our minds change to *think like him* (2 Corinthians 3:18).

First, we must get honest by examining our thoughts, our fears, and the images we hold of ourselves and the world in which we live.

Secondly, we approach the source of all knowledge, God himself, with our open and honest heart. Our prayer is *God, here I am. You know me better than I know myself. Please reveal to me what holds me back from progressing toward your full will and goal for my life.*

Such honesty transforms from the inside first. My prayer is that we are all transformed into the likeness of Jesus Christ (2 Corinthians 3:18). We cannot do this with our own wisdom and power. Only our supernatural God has such ability.

OVERCOMING FEAR

There is more evil in fear than
in the object that causes this fear.
—*Marcus Tullius Cicero*

Negative thoughts hamper our growth. These stem from negative emotions, especially fear. I am not referring to the fear necessary to self-preservation that allows us to avoid danger nor to the fear of the Lord, which keeps us from sin, but I refer to fears that keep us in a state of constant anxiety.

To obsess over a current situation or what could happen in the future saps us of any energy or creativity to live in the fullness God planned for us. Such fears come from the demonic realm, which is determined to rob us of our destiny.

Human nature feels compelled to mull over the same situations repeatedly. People who are ruled by fear think about past negative situations and convince themselves that the current one will end the same way. Chronically ill persons can relive every symptom of the past and paint dark images in their minds of the unknown future. They may tell themselves how unfortunate they are. Or, they may convince themselves that no one needs them. Such self-talk is based on fear. It paralyzes to the point that they cannot move forward with life.

Fears and worries vary, but the consequences remain unchanged: depression and destruction of the individual's destiny. Hence, these fears are sin. They cripple our potential and cause us to question God's goodness in our lives. They sap the energy that could be used toward creativity and development. When we encourage worry, it turns to destroys us.

Too many people live in the land of *what ifs,* so afraid of failing that they will not risk succeeding. Such constant fear of the unknown paralyzes them into living in limbo their entire lives.

The modern understanding of the word *sin* is wrongful deeds against God or others. However, the Greek word for sin (*hamartia*) means "to miss the mark." Like an inexperienced archer who over- or undershoots the target and misses it altogether, such is the original understanding of sin. God allows sin not for us to browbeat ourselves for how bad we are but for us to realize how far short of God's perfection and glory we fall.

Therefore, our missing the mark with God is not so much our failure through sin; rather, it is more about our failure to recognize our true potential as his sons and daughters. This error causes us to miss all we could be in Christ. It seems, instead, that the mark we miss is the mark of how great it can be, the prize we have in Him. Sin isn't how bad we are. It is how we fail to be who and what we could achieve—*in Christ.*

> ❝ Sin isn't how bad we are. It is how we fail to be who and what we could achieve—in Christ. ❞

Modern doctors have concluded that more than 87 percent of all illnesses can be attributed to the consequences of negative thinking, worry, and fear. The more one concentrates on a problem, the bigger the problem becomes, making it impossible to withstand the flood of self-created emotions. They feel worse, their thoughts darken, and eventually sickness manifests in their body. Constantly thinking about a problem worsens it. Incessant talking about a difficult situation does nothing to alleviate it; rather, it compounds it.

Job moaned, "For my sighing comes before I eat, and my groanings pour out like water. For the thing I greatly feared has come upon me and what I dreaded has happened to me" (Job 3:24, 25 NKJV). He realized that his miserable situation came due to his fears. The dread we harbor in our hearts and minds becomes our reality. Obviously, the words we speak reflect our soul's true condition.

LOVE CONQUERS FEAR

Our Life always expresses the result
of our dominant thoughts.
—Soren Kierkegaard

"There is no fear in love; but perfect love casts out fear, because fear involves torment. But he who fears has not been made perfect in love" (1 John 4:18 NKJV). Those trapped in the vicious cycle of fear may be wondering how to get out.

Imagine an empty glass. The only way to push air out of it is to fill it with liquid. Once the liquid overflows the rim, all the air is gone. So it is with God. Only the perfect love of Jesus displaces all fear.

Doesn't God encourage us against fear? "Fear not, for I am with you. Be not dismayed, for I am your God. I will strengthen you, yes, I will help you. I will uphold you with my righteous right hand" (Isaiah 41:10 NKJV). Those words are from the eternal God, not mortal man. They're either true or they're not.

Seymour Epstein, a well-known professor of psychology, remarked how people work hard to live healthy and prolong their lives by taking supplements, exercising regularly, and eating healthy and organic food. People do everything to avoid stress, lower their cholesterol, clean out blocked arteries, increase the capacity of their lungs, and try to avoid polluted atmosphere. However, in his opinion, thinking influences health more than any other factor.[8] In other words, fear and anxiety can actually cause physical harm to our bodies, no matter how many healthy choices we make.

How we think determines our future. Jot down every fear and negative thought that drives you. Take every one of them to God and place them in his hands. Only by acknowledging our fears and weakness can they lose the power and influence they've held over our lives. God's peace and confidence will fill our souls and hearts, propelling us toward the destiny he has set out for us.

THE POWER OF IMAGINATION

Our every thought creates our future.

—Louise Hay

Genesis records the fall of humankind when the serpent suggested to the woman that she would be as wise as God by eating what he forbade. She listened to his words, ate the fruit, and shared it with her husband (Genesis 3:4–6).

What happened?

First, the enemy sowed seeds of doubt in her mind and caused her to doubt the truth of God's words.

Second, he painted a glowing picture of what she would become by eating the fruit.

Finally, he directed her eyes to the object, tying her emotions to it. In an instant, she coveted God's wisdom of knowing both good and evil.

The enemy planted the seed that stimulated her imagination. That triggered emotions that caused her to act. From simply entertaining the enemy's suggestion came irreversible consequences.

Albert Einstein stated, "Imagination is more important than knowledge. For knowledge is limited, whereas imagination embraces the entire world."[9] Imagination is a powerful, God-given tool of creativity.

Imagination helps us conceive ideas as well as aiding in solving problems. It is organically connected to our thinking processes. Imagination helps lay out methodical solutions to situations.[10] It involves our emotions and helps us live life with more passion.

One evening, my wife and I decided to conduct a simple experiment with our children. They were tired, grumpy, and arguing among themselves. We called them into the living room.

"Do you remember our vacation last summer?" my wife asked.

"Yes!" they all responded. "It was wonderful."

"What did you enjoy the most?"

All three began speaking at one time, sharing their favorite memories. In moments, imagination transported all of us back to the warm beaches of Sarasota, Florida. They chattered about jumping the waves, collecting seashells, and building sandcastles. The atmosphere filled with joy as we all remembered that delightful time.

Memory triggers imagination that changes our mood and improves interpersonal relationships. It is capable of directing many psychological conditions and preparing us for upcoming endeavors. Willpower, fueled by imagination, can help us regulate breathing, slow the pulse, lower blood pressure, and reduce body temperature.

Once I went to visit a friend in the hospital. He'd broken his leg right at his knee. As he related the details of his accident and how much it hurt, I suddenly found myself feeling the same pain in my own knee.

As I listened to his story, my mind received the information he gave, sending a signal to my own body. Almost immediately, *my* knee began to ache. In that moment, I re-

ff Our minds cannot distinguish between reality and what our imagination conjures up. **JJ**

alized that our minds cannot distinguish between reality and what our imagination conjures up. Once emotion kicks in, we experience sympathy symptoms. Placing my attention on an area of pain produced the pain in my body.

Scientists have said that imagination is so powerful that sometimes the mind cannot distinguish between reality and imagination. Some years ago, a well-known Russian actor faced heart surgery. The doctors came in beforehand and drew out a heart on paper, explaining its function, what they anticipated accomplishing through surgery, and all risks. This actor, known for his lively imagination, listened intently to everything the physicians told him, including the risks—and promptly died. His imagination stopped his own heart.

A more positive example is George Hall, an airman shot down during the Vietnam War. For most of his 2,695 days in captivity, the North Vietnamese kept him locked in a small box. He maintained sanity by playing a full round of golf every day in his head. He felt the ball in his hand, teed up, chose his club, and made every hit in his imagination. One month after his release, he entered the New Orleans Open, and shot a 76.

If you imagine you will fail, you will. If you imagine you will succeed, you will do just that. Your imagination is that powerful. The enemy knows this fact and uses it constantly to drag us down and destroy our destiny.

The media feeds on fear, constantly spewing out bad news. Endless reports of tragedies all over the world fill the viewer with fear or anger at the great injustices. Christians can fall into this trap themselves by getting more caught up in the condition of the world rather than the supernatural power of God. This is exactly the goal of the enemy. Fatigue the believer, weaken his faith, and destroy purpose.

5-Max Felner, Unsplash

While Satan works on the mind for destruction, God uses our imagination for positive results. What our mind sees is far more powerful than what our natural eyes can. For example, God told Abram look up into heaven (Genesis 15:5) and count all the stars, promising that his descendants would be as numerous. Abram never saw his descendants with his natural eyes; rather, he saw them through the eyes of God—and believed. For this reason, he's considered a hero of faith because he believed what he couldn't see.

God promises that everything is possible to the one who believes. So watch your talk. Whatever is in your heart is what you will spend time talking about.

Eleanor Roosevelt is credited with saying, "Great minds discuss ideas. Average minds discuss events. Small minds discuss people." Check your conversation. Don't waste time talking about others or worrying what others may be saying about you. Save your thinking energy to create something significant for yourself or others. Accept God's challenge to gaze up at the sky and see your future written there—by him.

Remember, emotions are tied to our imagination. If we imagine sickness or accidents or failure, emotion kicks in and fuels the fire of panic. Often, the very thing we feared happens, not because God wanted it, but we imagined our way into it. Have you ever said to yourself, *I knew I'd fail that test?* You succeeded in that failure, didn't you? Why? What you'd determined in your heart became your truth and the reality.

How would your life change if you imagined Jesus standing right next to you? Even in the most difficult times, knowing his promise to never leave or forsake you would propel you forward because that imagination becomes your reality.

Our minds are so amazing. They file every thought and every event, any of which can be brought up into memory at any time. If you fill your files with fears and failures, that is all that can be retrieved later. Instead, fill your files with God's truth. Those are the ones that will surface in times of crisis.

Imagination creates every piece of music, every sculpture, every building, every automobile. The imagination of the Creator became their reality and manifested in the finished product.

The same holds true for the lack of imagination. If you tell yourself you can't succeed at your job or you'll never find a mate or you're too old to start over—you're probably right. Some refer to this as self-fulfilling prophecy. Watch your words. Guard your thoughts.

PROTECT YOUR HEART

The absence of foolish thoughts means
the absence of foolish deeds.
—Kun-Tsy

A young mother began a journal after the birth of her first child. In it, she recorded continuous nightmares that involved herself and the baby. Every dream held a common theme of disaster: death, accidents, their home destroyed by fire. She allowed her imagination to run unchecked and spent many hours weeping.

The birth of a child is an extremely important time in any woman's life. It should be a time of great joy. However, this lady entertained dark thoughts for so long, she lost the ability to control her emotions. Fortunately, she sought and received help for the physical aspect of her situation.

Medication may help rebalance our bodies, but cannot alter our thought life. Should the lady fail to learn how to control her thoughts, she could lose out on destiny. Negative thoughts must be stopped before they settle into our spirit and become convictions.

As Martin Luther said, "You cannot keep birds from flying over your head but you can keep them from building a nest in your hair." Fleeting undesirable thoughts do no harm. It's when we continue to replay negative words, situations, or worries in our heads that they enter into our hearts. Then they settle into our consciousness and our soul (emotion, mind, and will).

The Bible tells us to guard our hearts because out of it comes our hopes, fears, successes or failures (Proverbs 4:23). We need to guard against negativity that will stifle and destroy us. When a negative emotion arises, we should take that as a warning to deal with it.

Perhaps you were hurt by someone you loved. The hurt is legitimate. It happened. Perhaps you spend hours rehashing this moment in your mind or you often complain of what happened to others. Such constant obsessing moves from negative thoughts and settles into the subconscious, turning into conviction. By reliving the trauma and refusing to forgive the perpetrator, you derail your own destiny.

Is it possible to relearn thinking? This is a serious question that will require real work to make happen. We cannot change our thought life without first rejecting the old way of thinking. We must dig into God's Word to replace every negative, long-held lie with *his* truth.

Did your father tell you that you'd never amount to anything? Did it settle so deep into your spirit that it has become part of your identity? What is *God's* truth? He calls you his own dear son (1 John 3:1). You are so valuable to him that he takes the time to count the hairs on your head (Luke 12:7). He's compassionate, even in your weaknesses (Psalm 103:13, 14).

Did your spouse abuse you and call you worthless? What does God's Word say? He says for you to not be afraid. He will remove your shame, and *he* will be your husband (Isaiah 54). He says you are no longer deserted, but his delight (Isaiah 62:4).

Embrace what God declares about you and stop agreeing with the lies of the enemy. This takes effort, especially if you've been believing such lies for many years. Confess your own weakness and ask God to infuse you with his supernatural strength.

Anyone can take the easy way by going with the flow. However, one never reaches his purpose this way. It takes strength and courage to battle the norm and achieve destiny. God is ready to help anyone who loves him with his whole heart, longs to live for and serve

> It takes strength and courage to battle the norm and achieve destiny.

him, and wants intimate fellowship with him. Declare God's promises out loud. Keep your mind set on Christ, never on circumstances.

As you listen to messages of encouragement, surround yourself with people who will not only help you build your faith but keep you accountable for negative thoughts and actions.

Another way to overcome damaging words or events is to rejoice. Paul urges his Philippian readers to rejoice multiple times. Keep in mind that he wrote to them while sitting in prison. How could he rejoice? Only through his intimate connection with God.

Rejoice! The enemy can't take joy. Read the Bible out loud. Pray out loud. Play worship music. He will flee because he can't stand it. You will not only defeat the enemy, but more importantly, you will improve your mental, spiritual, and physical health.

Here are a few points for changing your thought patterns:

- Take responsibility for what you think. Don't blame circumstances or the actions and words of others for your struggle.

- Be honest with yourself.

- Think high thoughts, such as the vastness of the God you love and serve.

- Start with small steps.

- Communicate with others who are strong in their walk of faith and who can lift you up, not tear you down.

- Find joy.

Seek the positive in everything. "It could've been worse" is a good start. Find joy even in difficult situations. Great opposition is great opportunity to gain priceless communion with God.

Did you know that your spirit accepts all your thoughts as truth? Be careful to not allow offense, fear, or discouragement from settling into your spirit where they will reside in the subconscious and are harder to root out. Remember, thoughts matter, because thoughts *are* matter.

ALTER YOUR DNA

Our every thought creates our future.

—Louise L. Hay

"The Lord said to Abram, 'Look around from where you are, to the north and south, to the east and west. All the land that you see I will give to you and your offspring forever'" (Genesis 13:14–15 NIV). He reiterated that promise in Genesis 15:5 (NKJV): "Look now towards heaven, and count the stars if you are able to number them… So shall your descendants be."

God commanded Abraham (still called Abram at this time) to meditate on the number of stars in the sky, as well as the grains of sand beneath his feet. He needed to stretch Abraham's imagination before he could bless him. To do this, he had to teach him that blessings come through faith.

God used various situations to develop Abraham's faith. He wanted him to become a human channel through which countless other souls would be blessed. Abraham had no children when God told him to count the stars. Physically, he was an old man. However, as his confidence in God grew, he could imagine each star as a child. Every bit of sand represented offspring.

He *saw* the multitude of his descendants over his head and under his feet. His imagination produced faith, and that faith changed impossible to possible. God wants his children to have his faith, God kind of faith (Mark 11:22–23). God's faith operates differently. He sees and declares the end from the beginning (Isaiah 46:10). When we see the desired end and are fully convinced that what we say comes to pass, then we declare the end into being. Arm yourself with an absolute picture of what God desires for you, imagine it to be true, and experience it as a reality. Thank God for that. Then the joy associated with the end result becomes an abiding re-ality; you have now harmonized your soul (mind, emotions, and the will).

Not only does God push us to imagine the impossible, he also provides the strategy to make it happen. Jacob's father-in-law made a deal with Jacob (Genesis 30:25–43). He agreed Jacob could take all the sheep that were speckled, streaked, or spotted for his wages. Then he stole all those sheep and moved his herds three days away.

> ❝ Abraham's imagination produced faith, and that faith changed impossible to possible. ❞

Instead of seeking re-venge, Jacob thought of a creative way to cause the ewes to birth only speck-led, spotted, and streaked lambs through stripping the saplings of green poplar, almond, and chestnut trees and sticking them in the ground where the flocks watered.

Next, Jacob interbred those sheep until their strain was the strongest and the other sheep the weakest. How did he come up with such creativity?

Through God. He taught Jacob important facts of structure of human life using genetic principles of his flock. Through this strategy, Jacob al-tered the DNA of each sheep. God can do the same with humanity. Creative thought, coupled with faith in God, empowers us to change our own DNA. "A cell's life is controlled by the physical and energetic environment and not by its genes. It is a single cell's awareness of the environment, not its genes, that sets into motion the mechanisms of life."[11] "Our thought and our feelings are the blueprints, the energetic encoding, for our lives. With our thoughts and feelings we influence the world around us; we alter the physical function of our bodies; and we ever reprogram our cells."[12]

Remember, when we think, our thoughts emit an electrical and mag-netic energy into our bodies and the world around us. Increasing the emotion is like increasing the electromagnetic influence on the subatomic world. We are the sum total of our thoughts, emotions, and words. Every person moves in the image they have of themselves in their mind. If you fill your thoughts with images of success and health, you naturally gravitate toward situations and life decisions that ensure its completion. Just like the Russian actor and the American POW, the human mind cannot distinguish between real life experience and vivid imagination. Whatever the mind sees, the body accepts. Whatever we plant in our subconscious is validated through repetition and nourished with emotion, and will one day become reality.

Negative images such as news reports of natural disasters, terror attacks, and other catastrophes can trigger adverse emotions of fear, anger, or depression. Once we allow those emotions to settle in our souls, we threaten our joy, peace of mind, and close relationships. This is exactly the enemy's plan— to rob us of God's plan for our lives and sidetrack us with pointless worry.

> **"** Whatever we plant in our subconscious is validated through repetition and nourished with emotion, and will one day become reality. **"**

How you view yourself determines how you will live. If you dare to imagine success, victory, and health (God's desires for you), you will move toward achieving the same. If you allow doubts and fears to rule your thoughts, what you fear will become your reality. We are not victims of our genes. With God's help and the work of the Holy Spirit, you will be able to alter your DNA.

All thoughts are stored in memory, which the brain can recall upon demand. Memory stores the data of past thoughts and experience. It has the capability of combining your thoughts and experiences in limitless ways. Many discoveries in the technical and scientific world are based on right combinations of already existing elements or previous inventions.

The engineer puts together elements already in his conscious or subconscious mind to create something new. The musician combines notes, sounds, and ideas already nestled in his memory to compose a new piece. Preexisting thoughts give birth to new buildings, music, and ideas.

The same holds true for negative memory. Harbored thoughts of fear, doubt, and envy generate more of the same. Those entrenched emotions lead to strongholds.

STRONGHOLDS

If you do not conquer self,

you will be conquered by self.

—*Napoleon Hill*

I once met an interesting young man whom I liked from the start. He seemed to have everything going for him: intelligence, talent, education. He lacked nothing. Yet, as our friendship continued, he never progressed into what he clearly could accomplish. Some invisible barrier prevented him from being the total person God intended.

I realized this young man had strongholds in his life. The Bible addresses this in 2 Corinthians 10:4–5 (NIV): "The weapons we fight with are not the weapons of the world. On the contrary, they have divine power to demolish strongholds. We demolish arguments and every pretension that sets itself up against the knowledge of God, and we take captive every thought to make it obedient to Christ."

Take captive every thought. That's God's command to us because he knows that we either capture our thoughts or they capture us. When our thoughts control us, they become a stronghold of preconceived ideas, like a fortress or prison, down in our deepest being that shuts out our ability to receive God's revelation or will. This spiritual incarceration robs us of any freedom in our spirit or soul. We cannot delight in all the privileges God's kingdom offers. Jesus Christ cannot be fully Lord of our lives as long as the fortress keeps our minds bound up.

We must gain power over negative thoughts. To do so requires learning new skills.

- Develop a strong work ethic (Ephesians 4:28).

- Speak only pure and wholesome language (Ephesians 4:29).

- Always tell the truth (Ephesians 4:25).

God reveals His law of renewal in the above verses. It's impossible to think and do things in new ways without first rejecting the old. We won't work until we've stopped stealing. We must eliminate foul language before we can fill our mouths with virtuous conversation.

Strongholds twist truth. Consequently, we begin believing the lies of the enemy and living out of that perception. If we believe that nobody cares about us or that we are a failure, then we will become convinced in the deepest part of our heart that we are, indeed, inferior. No matter how talented we are or how pleasant our personality, we view our self through the lens of our own inferiority complex, and no one can talk us out of that misperception.

Old hurts turn into strongholds when we entertain them and refuse to release them into God's hands. No matter how much we may want to change, it always seems just out of reach. The walls are too high, too daunting. For many, this is a daily battle in the spirit realm. Regardless, it is a battle well worth fighting, for it brings us closer to God's truth and our destiny in him.

Forget the past. Refuse to linger in the pain, the disappointment, the slander, or abuse. Press *forward* to the high calling of God (Philippians 3:13). We cannot change the past, but our future lies before us, to be shaped by our thoughts and actions.

The only possible way to win absolute control over negative thoughts is to replace them with God's Word. He tells us he has a purpose for us, a future, and a hope (Jeremiah 29:11) He promises to never leave nor forsake us

> The only possible way to win absolute control over negative thoughts is to replace them with God's Word.

(Hebrews 13:5). The Creator proclaims that there is nothing impossible for Him. His Word is filled with promises for us. Replace every negative thought about yourself and your circumstances with what God says. Believe his ability to solve any problem.

The Lord is ready to help anyone who loves him with his whole heart, lives for him, and serves him. Prayer opens our minds and hearts to trust him. Make declarations over your life, using verses from the Bible, to help you keep your thoughts in God's stream and not be subject to the waves of doubt that can engulf your spirit and soul. Listen to sermons that encourage and strengthen your trust in God. Communicate with other people of faith who can admonish and encourage you.

Time spent in God's presence shapes us and is, therefore, worth any struggle in the physical realm. Each morning, put your trust in our eternal, unchanging God rather than in any temporary situation that may be swirling around you. Let joy be your strength (Nehemiah 8:10).

The enemy wants you to fail, but God desires your success. Anchoring yourself in his word helps you understand the seen and unseen worlds through God's viewpoint. If you dwell in his glory, you will grow in his strength. Your thoughts will change from helpless negativity to joyful anticipation.

Pray this: Dear heavenly Father, I thank you for this weapon of imagination that you gave me to destroy all the strongholds the enemy has planted in my mind. Open my eyes to see your truth. I trust you. Let your word take root in my heart and mind. I renounce all false convictions that were planted in me with or without my knowledge. Destroy those false convictions and all other strongholds by the blood of Jesus Christ. Destroy any evil root and free me from everything that holds me from walking in the fullness of your promises. As I receive your forgiveness for my past negative thought life, I will embrace your destiny for me in the name of Jesus. Amen."

THOUGHTS FOR REFLECTION

1. Write down and confront all negative thoughts and fears. Then, destroy them!

2. How can I stop negative thoughts?

3. Which strongholds are holding me back?

4. Which of God's promises do I hold closest to my heart? Write them down and reflect on them daily.

<u>Step 3</u>

EMOTIONS

Environment becomes Thoughts — Thoughts --→ **EMOTIONS** — Emotions --→ Words
Words --→ Actions — Actions --→ Habits — Habits --→ Character
Character becomes your
DESTINY

Five emotions hinder our lives:
pride, envy, anger, pity, and fear.
—Unknown

It looks like rain.

One day as I crossed the bridge over the Columbia River, I noticed the overcast skies. They quickly changed from soft gray to dark, angry clouds, scudding across the horizon.

It's going to pour.

Soon, raindrops pelted against my windshield, and I flipped the wipers on.

I'll get soaked if this doesn't let up before I get home. The clouds turned deep black as the rain increased.

This is awful. The outdoor chill seemed to seep into the car, though I had the heater set to a comfortable temperature.

I forgot to make that call I promised. I need to clean the garage. The family's coming over. I should have done it yesterday. And, I need to call about that bill.

Suddenly, I found myself thinking a multitude of gloomy thoughts. Daily problems grew bigger. More daunting. Petty situations loomed large. The distress in my heart increased.

What happened? I had allowed my soul to take on the environment around me. Emotions are like the weather. Sunny emotions make us feel lighter, happier, while woeful ones push our spirit down. Such unchecked thoughts can even cause physical illness. In this chapter, we will explore the importance of controlling our emotions, rather than allowing them to control us.

THE PROSPEROUS SOUL

Tranquility is stronger than emotions.
Silence louder than shouts.
Indifference more frightening than war.
—Unknown

The human body needs water, food, air, and rest to function properly. In the same manner, our soul needs love, acceptance, and peace. We often forget this, so we neglect our soul's health through not feeding it good and wholesome emotions.

Some people actually teach that to be truly spiritual, one must suppress or ignore such needs to focus totally on the spiritual. Yet the apostle John wrote to Gaius, "I pray that in all respects you may prosper and be in good health, just as your soul prospers" (3 John 2 NKJV). Note that prosperity and health are *directly related* to the soul.

Many sermons focus on how to become more spiritual. However, few aim at how to manage the soul. We must know how to master our emotions, mind, and will to positively influence our lives. I've heard and agree with this expression: "Our emotions are great passengers but terrible drivers." What are emotions? They are the immediate sensations we feel the moment we face any situation, positive or negative. Emotions are always associated with direct experiences and may, consequently, affect our destiny.

You just ran a red light. Fear rushes through your body. Your knees weaken, and your heart pounds.

I could have caused an accident. Is there an officer nearby? Will I get a ticket? How much will it cost?

This is an *immediate* reaction to a current event.

Established emotions manifest through feelings. Long-term feelings settle in a person's soul. Take the feeling of love, for example. A young man and woman fall in love and marry. Their feelings are strong and deep for one another. After a few years, she may get frustrated when she finds his dirty socks in the middle of the floor while

> ❝ Our emotions are great passengers but terrible drivers. ❞

he may have a flash of anger the moment he picks up a new tube of toothpaste to find that she has squeezed it from the middle. The stronger feeling of love, however, will overrule the temporary emotion because it has grown from a shared history. Strong, loving feelings cause the relationship to mature and prosper. Shallow and selfish ones sprout irritations capable of growing out of proportion and killing the relationship. When there is conflict between a thought and a feeling, the feeling always prevails. Also, when there is conflict between will power and a feeling, the feeling will take over.

I once talked to a young man who confided that every time his basketball team lost, he experienced irrational anger. He became discouraged when the players failed to meet his expectations. During the course of our conversation, it became clear that the feelings were not caused by how his team played. Rather, each loss was perceived by him as a personal failure. The roots of those emotions ran deep into his childhood from rejection by his father.

6-Dani Vivanco, Unsplash

Personal emotional experience creates our own unique perception of life. Molded through interpersonal relationships, each shapes our core values and aspirations, thus affecting our future.

For this reason, the enemy works hard to control our minds. He uses our uncontrolled emotions to plant strategic lies, designed to strip us of hope. Because the mind accepts negative thoughts more readily than positive, those thoughts can multiply into a destructive force that binds us and obliterates our destiny.

When a baby elephant is born, the handlers chain one leg to a peg. No matter how hard he tugs, he cannot release himself. After a while, he comes to believe escape is impossible, so he stops struggling. After he reaches maturity, he could pull out the stake with a quick lift of his leg, but he's so programmed that he never even tries.

Such is the goal of the enemy—to keep our minds chained to lies when we could easily be free. Once he has located an overriding lie that we believe or one we are willing to entertain in our thoughts he *will* most definitely build a fortress there. He uses those pivotal points with cunning strategy.

The human mind is programmed to believe the negative. Pessimism is extremely contagious. For this reason, the enemy will try to put people in your life who have the ability to instill fear and doubt. The goal is to get you to *quit*.

> **ƒƒ** Over 90 percent of what people fear never happens. **ƒƒ**

Once we've allowed those lies to settle into your mind and heart, they become strongholds in both our conscious and subconscious state. This takes a huge emotional toll on us. We must understand his tactics to develop immunity against them.

Our thought life affects our physical health, how we live our daily lives, our relationships, and our decisions. For example, the fear of rejection hinders us from developing close friendships. Fear of the future blocks our ability to function as God wants us to in order to prosper. Fear of failure prevents any possibility of success and fulfillment in life.

Fear paralyzes the mind. It makes us see a fly as an elephant and a kitten as a tiger. Fear also takes past negative experiences and projects them into the future. I've learned that over 90 percent of what people fear *never happens*. For this reason, we must hand over all our thoughts to God and trust in his strength and goodness—not in our emotions.

Because fear disables us from moving forward, God tells us not to fear at least 365 times in the Bible—one for every day of the year. A personal favorite is Isaiah 41:10 (NKJV): "Fear not, for I am with you; be not dismayed, for I am your God; I will strengthen you, yes, I will help you, I will uphold you with my righteous right hand."

Take God at his word. Embrace his love and protecting hand on your life. Live for him and your family with joyful love. Trust the Lord and *fear not!*

Take a moment to reflect on your life. Which emotions dominate? Do you remember the last time you felt loved? Enjoyed the sun? Listened to the birds singing outside your window? Heard a good sermon?

Or, is the only thing you remembered from that message the baby fussing behind you?

THE INNER BOMB

One of the biggest weaknesses is
to let feelings take over.
—Unknown

Our emotions directly affect our destiny. Moses had a serious problem with anger. He murdered an Egyptian guard whom he saw abusing his people. As a result, he escaped to a desert place where God took forty years to work on his heart. Soon after Israel's liberation, Moses returned from face-to-face communion with God to find his people worshiping an idol. He became so enraged he *broke* the two stone tablets. Later, God told him to speak to a rock to release water to the people. Frustrated with the people's constant complaints, he flew into another rage and beat on the rock with his shepherd's staff.

That act of unrestrained anger cost him his place in the Promised Land. Although God allowed him to see it from a distance, he could not enter. He lost the biggest opportunity of his life because he failed to control his emotions. Anger, guilt, and shame are incredibly destructive emotions that become self-fulfilling prophecies.

Christians are no more immune to anger than the rest of humankind. It is an emotion God placed in us at creation. "In your anger do not sin. Do not let the sun go down while you are still angry" (Ephesians 4:26 NIV).

> **ff** Moses lost the biggest opportunity of his life because he failed to control his emotions. **JJ**

Anger alone is not sin. It can be likened to temptation (James 1:14–15). One only sins by yielding to the temptation, not by feeling the temptation itself. I can see a beautiful car and start calculating how to afford it. If I come to the conclusion that I cannot afford it, I have not sinned. However, if I yield to what *I want* and put my family into financial difficulties, I have most certainly turned that temptation into sin.

We live in a society driven by anger. Road rage, racial tensions, and frustration over workplace inequality are serious issues we all face. Those emotions can easily spill over into anger toward momentary inconveniences, such as waiting at an extra-long traffic signal, burned toast, or stubbing a toe.

The physical reaction is the same for both serious problems and temporary ones. Anger pumps adrenaline into our system and causes the sympathetic nervous system to become agitated. Blood pressure rises. Small ulcers develop in the duodenal intestine.

Anger by itself is not a sin. It's a warning signal for the body to take action. How we choose to handle the anger determines whether it becomes sin. If I see a child being bullied, anger flashes through me as I rush to help him. That is not sin but rather constructive anger mobilized because of injustice. However, if I beat the bully senseless, that's a sin because I allowed the anger to control me to the point of destructive action.

Uncontrolled anger can even kill. I read an article about a man who'd left his toddler alone for a few minutes. When he returned, he saw the boy had pushed over the TV and found it broken on the floor. In a rage, the man kicked his young son in the stomach. The boy died 24 hours later from internal bleeding. His father asked for no leniency from the judge. No pardon. He only wished to attend the funeral to say goodbye to the child his anger had killed.

Author June Hunt likens sudden anger to a ferocious fire-breathing dragon that spreads fear through the ones we love the most. She explains that the only effective "dragon slayer" is dwelling in God's presence, the place where he fills our hearts with peace.[13]

She also states that to deal with anger, one must know the root causes. She names four:

- hurt
- injustice
- fear
- frustration

Only when we know the root of our anger can we work to overcome it with God's power.

"My dear brothers and sisters, take note of this: Everyone should be quick to listen, slow to speak and slow to become angry" (James 1:19 NIV). Patience diffuses anger. I love to barbecue steaks. After properly marinating them, I adjust the flame on the grill. Too high and the meat turns to charcoal. Too little and I get a dried out, tough steak. It takes patience and experience to control the fire. James is telling his readers to be patient.

ANGER KILLS HEALTH

Anger and intolerance are the
enemies of correct understanding.
—Mahatma Gandhi

In both anger and stress, the adrenal glands pump extra adrenaline throughout the body, which produces agitation in the sympathetic nervous system. Blood pressure increases. The skin pales. Small ulcers pop up in the duodenal intestine. Those ulcers heal quickly once the cause of the stress is resolved. However, under prolonged stress or anger, the ulcers remain. It is necessary to dissipate the adrenaline for the physiological process to work properly.

King Solomon admonishes his readers to control their anger through patience. "He who is slow to anger is better than the mighty, and he who rules his spirit than he who takes a city" (Proverbs 16:32 NKJV).

> **"** "He who is slow to anger is better than the mighty, and he who rules his spirit than he who takes a city" (Proverbs 16:32 NKJV). **"**

The ability to manage our emotions is a major key to success. Any achievement is useless if the person cannot overcome himself. Angry people act foolishly (Proverbs 14:17). They stir up strife. They sin through their rage (Proverbs 29:22).

Be careful of building friendships with people who cannot control their anger (Proverbs 22:24–25). Like an ocean wave, anger can build slowly, underwater and unseen, as it races toward the shore. Once it hits land, all the built up energy crashes with destructive fury. If we allow anger to simmer long enough, it will increase to the point where we explode, crashing harmful words over those closest to our heart. This is what the writer of Hebrews explains.

> "Pursue peace with all people, and holiness, without which no one will see the Lord: looking carefully lest anyone fall short of the grace of God; lest any root of bitterness springing up cause trouble, and by this many become defiled" (Hebrews 12:14–15 NKJV).

Deal with anger quickly, before the day's end. Do not carry it over to the next day and allow it to build into a deadly force.

God has designed humans to carry only the problems of *today*. Jesus instructed his disciples not to worry about tomorrow. Focus only on today because today is all we are promised (Matthew 6:34).

My personal three-day rule is this: Deal with yesterday, exercise sound judgment for today's decisions, and look forward to tomorrow with hope. Resolve yesterday's issues so they do not become a heavy burden to you. Do not let the problems of the past affect your present. Leave them with God and move forward. Otherwise, the past infects the present and hijacks the future.

❝ My personal three-day rule is this: Deal with yesterday, exercise sound judgment for today's decisions, and look forward to tomorrow with hope. ❞

Unresolved issues hinder the restful sleep we need to operate at peak performance physically, mentally, emotionally, and spiritually. Through the quality of our feeling and beliefs, we create our health and our quality of life!

DEALING WITH ANGER

Speak when you are angry
and you'll make the best speech
you'll ever regret.
—Laurence J. Peter

Joseph M. Stowell III, president of Cornerstone University, wrote in his article "My Tongue is My Enemy" that to be "slow to anger" means holding it until you have time to evaluate its source. Determine the source of your anger before letting it flare up like an uncontrolled fire. He goes on to state ways to help one control the anger and solve the problem.

First, ask yourself, Why am I angry? If it's in response to correction, be humble enough to accept it. Or, perhaps your life is so disorganized, you lost your temper because of frustration. Be honest enough to admit your own shortcomings before focusing on those of other people.

Were you tired? Unmotivated to do what you needed to do? Did your sudden rage hide feelings of guilt, fear, or disappointment?

Did the other person violate your rights? If so, humbly allow God to handle the situation because he instructs us not to repay evil with evil (Romans 12:17–21).

Did anger overtake you from a past situation with other people? This is called transference, and it's unjust to punish anyone for the mistakes of others. Nursing past hurts causes bitterness to anchor in your soul and defile it.

"Watch over each other to make sure that no one misses the revelation of God's grace. And make sure no one lives with a root of bitterness sprouting within them which will only cause trouble and poison the hearts of many" (Hebrews 12:15 TPT).

Second, do you have a right to be angry? God asked Jonah why he was angry. God wanted to show mercy on Nineveh. That

> 66 Nursing past hurts causes bitterness to anchor in your soul and defile it. 99

angered Jonah because his heart was not right. He needed to submit to God's will and turn his attitude into mercy rather than vengeance.

Third, determine if your anger is driven by self-pity. Such was the case in Luke 15:31, in the story of the prodigal son. The elder felt sorry for himself rather than rejoicing that his brother came home. As difficult as it can be to "Rejoice with those who rejoice" (Romans 12:15 NIV) during our own hard times, it's an opportunity to grow in God's grace.

Fourth, take time to cool down. This one step alone could save yourself and the object of your anger much heartache from hasty words. In the moment that rage struggles to master you, go for a walk. Talk to God. Tell him everything that's upsetting you. Get a punching bag if you need a more aggressive means to release the wrath inside you. The release of negative energy through forceful physical activity will release the built-up adrenaline flow and bring the body to a state of peace.

Be aware that these activities will bring only temporary relief for an ongoing problem. However, it is most important to diffuse the anger before seeking a permanent solution.

Fifth, try to look at the situation from a different perspective. Put yourself in the other person's place. Try to understand why he said what he said or did what he did. The Bible calls this gentleness (see Galatians 5:22–23).

If you do not understand why you're angry, be honest. Talk it through with a person you trust until you understand your personal triggers.[14] This alone would save much grief between spouses. The same holds true for parents and children. Always, always exercise patience. Counting to ten will help us choose gentle, soothing words over lashing out.

Deal with all anger issues before retiring for the night so your body can relax and allow sleep to renew its energy. Fall asleep meditating on God's goodness and forgiveness. This gives us inner peace and heals our souls.

HOPE IS A GOD-GIVEN TOOL

You think that your life is tough?
Start helping someone whose life is worse than yours.
—Unknown

If anger is not crippling you, perhaps depression is. Depressed persons become so preoccupied with their circumstances that it is impossible to find relief. Depression lowers productivity and quality of life. The World Health Organization (WHO) estimates the U.S. economy suffers the loss of one trillion dollars annually because of depression or anxiety in workers, who either quit their jobs rather than deal with issues or seek medical attention and time off from work to do so. By 2020, depression is expected to become the number one killer in our country, especially among young people, as more and more people commit suicide. It has often been said that suicide "is a permanent solution to a temporary problem."

Like other negative issues, depression is contagious. Put a seriously depressed person in a room full of people, and after a short while of listening to their complaints, everyone else rushes to tell how difficult their own situation is. Before long, *everybody* is infected with depression. The more we complain, the worse we feel. The worse we feel, the more opportunity we have to slip into the enemy's trap of complete hopelessness.

Depression is contagious. Constant mulling over a situation will not only infect you, it will contaminate everyone around you. Thus, you hold the power to destroy not only your own life but those of others as well.

> ❝ When we allow hope to dwell inside our innermost being, our imagination develops possibilities for a better future and connects us to the divine plan. ❞

How does one move from an existence of defeat to living in victory? Jesus invites us to come to him, "...all you who labor and are heavy laden, and I will give you rest" (Matthew 11:28 NKJV). Only a close and open relationship with God solves the problem of depression. Paul wrote that no matter how difficult a situation may be, it is only temporary. Only what transpires in the spirit realm remains eternal (2 Corinthians 4:16–18).

We must entrust our lives to our great, almighty, and all-knowing God, realizing that *everything* is in His hands. Only one touch of his grace changes any situation. Once we understand the depth of God's love and power, our thinking becomes transformed. We put all our hope in him, which strengthens our faith (Hebrews 6:19).

Hope is a God-given tool. He uses hope to form our future. When we allow hope to dwell inside our innermost being, our imagination develops possibilities for a better future. As we imagine ourselves experiencing a goal, we will identify the associated emotions. Hope shapes your methods of traversing your current situation. "The cognitions associated with hope—how you think when you are hopeful—are pathways to desired goals and reflect a motivation to pursue goals (Snyder, Harris, Anderson, & Holleran, 1991). Better problem-solving abilities have been found in people who are hopeful when compared with low-hope peers (Change, 1998), and those who are hopeful have a tendency to be cognitively flexible and able to mentally explore novel situations (Breznitz, 1986)."[15] Hope finds the way out. Hope creates new paths and connects us with our future. Through meditation we have the ability to experience an event before it actually happens. Sometimes previewing can help us develop emotional impressions. God converts those impressions into a blueprint to map out our destiny. Hope anchors us to that divine plan.

Allow God to take you from any pit by painting his picture on the canvas of your heart. Trust him and hold that picture close. It can and will change your destiny.

INNER PEACE — OUTER CALM

The mind is the eye of the soul, not its strength.
The strength of the soul is in the heart.
—Unknown

We live in an age of speed. As I visit larger cities, I physically feel the stress in the atmosphere as people hurry about. People walk fast and drive fast, showing no patience for the casual ambler. I've found the opposite true in small towns. People are quick to engage in conversation with a friend or stranger.

According to some statistics, more than 90 percent of our population experience daily stress[16]. Stress is so common, it is now considered the norm of life. Many folks unconsciously become agitated should they suddenly find themselves without anything to do in any given time.

Research has proven that after a person has reached a certain stress level, the mind isolates itself from prerecorded information in the heart.[17] In other words, the person loses the ability to hear their own heart, which serves as our inner compass. This communications shutdown can lead to rash and unwise decisions.

The routine of unrelenting stressful living takes a toll on rest. Rest is more than mere sleep. Rest rejuvenates the spirit and soul as well as the body. Rest renews the cells of our body and recharges the mind. Rest helps us hear God's voice in our heart.

We are bombarded with countless decisions every day. In an environment of constant stress, we rely on the intellect of our mind rather than God's voice in our heart. Mind-choices do not always line up with God's best for us, for busyness and stress often deaden our ability to hear him.

It is imperative to create an atmosphere of calm before important decisions. Quiet your soul. Pray. Listen to worship music. Set aside all your own ambitions and ask for God's will in what you face. He knows what is best for you.

Jesus understood the challenges of the human experience when he walked among us. After watching many stressing out about life, he offered an invitation to come to him and receive his supernatural rest (Matthew 11:28).

Many doctors recognize that persons of faith react less to stress. Their trust in God keeps their psychological and physical health stabilized. While medications are necessary to cope with some forms of depression, they cannot solve the issues of the soul. Only faith in God can exchange sorrow for joy. Only he can turn mourning into laughter (Jeremiah 31:13, John 16:20).

David talked to himself when he got depressed. Rather than focus on the negative, he said, "Why are you cast down, O my soul, and why are you in turmoil within me?" (Psalm 42:11 ESV). He then answers his own question in the same verse: "Hope in God; for I shall again praise him, my salvation and my God."

We must learn to control our emotions, or they *will* control us. Remember that everything seen in the natural is *temporary*, while the unseen is *eternal*. Only by entrusting our lives to our great, almighty, and all-knowing God can we enjoy peace. This perspective transforms our thinking, brings us hope, and strengthens our faith. Like David, we must *command* our soul to trust in God.

I have a friend who likes to say, "A true master of the house is not the one who can put his house in order: it's the one who can keep disorder *out*." We cannot always control our circumstances, but we do have the responsibility to identify our emotions, bring them under God's authority, and adjust them with our destiny in mind. That is why God orders us to guard our hearts (Proverbs 4:23).

Those persons who put all their faith in God know their future is secure because it rests in God. Good times, bad times—they know that nothing takes God by surprise. They remain confident because they know their Creator on an intimate level.

The optimist turns every failure into a growth opportunity. The pessimist expects the worst to happen. When it does, the response is tired vindication: "See? I told you so." Remember, both the dreams of the optimist and the nightmares of the pessimist become reality—all because of the power of the mind.

THE TURNAROUND

Faith is taking the first step
even when you don't see
the whole staircase.
—Martin Luther King, Jr.

How can I change my natural inclinations for negative thinking into those of hope? Denial accomplishes nothing. We must acknowledge all the hurts, fears, and disappointments that drove us into the cycle of negativity.

Next, we must resolve to change, first by talking to God about it, then searching out his plans, promises, and purposes in the Bible. Meditate on his words. Find an accountability partner—a member of your family or a friend—who will encourage you and lovingly keep you on track.

Music is a well-known technique for therapy. Fill your ears and heart with worship music that will settle in your heart and strengthen your faith. As Paul wrote, "Sing and make music from your heart to the Lord" (Ephesians 5:19 NIV).

Active participation in worship transforms our feelings. It positively influences the human spirit. David calmed Saul's soul through singing and playing his psalms (1 Samuel 16:23). We communicate with God and he communicates with us through music. Let every song become a prayer of your soul.

Hobbies also help de-stress us and give us something to focus on other than what depresses us. Creating things releases more of the creativity God implanted in us and consequently brings hope and joy.

If certain thoughts or memories dominate your thinking, take some time to analyze them. For example, if you lost your job, don't focus on the loss. Think about hidden opportunities. Should you change careers? Go back to school?

Remind yourself that many successful people experienced the same loss and used it as a stepping-stone for a better future. Focus your thoughts on the positives that still remain. Your health. Family. Friends. Be humble enough to ask for their help as you transition to a new phase.

A new perspective on any situation changes our feelings. We simply need to understand why we dwell on specific memories and then ask God to help us change them from hopeless to hopeful. At first, you may consider it a daunting task, but with God, anything is possible (Matthew 19:26).

HAPPINESS IS THE BEST MEDICINE

Laughter is the sun that drives
winter from the human face.
—Victor Hugo

Get happy. I grew up during a difficult time in my home country. Often, my elders quoted a verse to me, "The righteous seldom smile." Serious faces and attitudes surrounded me. Imagine my shock when I tried to find this verse in the Bible after I grew up! Through this experience I learned that it was impossible to relax when I concentrated on my family's struggles. However, when I turned to God for answers, he taught me to praise him in the *middle* of trying situations.

Is it possible to be happy when life is difficult and not everything turns out as we wish? So often, I meet people who tell me about their problems, debts, or sicknesses. These people are so focused on their difficulties that they cannot relax. They fail to see all the beauty of life around them. Naturally, some situations require a span of time for resolution. However, this is no excuse for entertaining depression.

Start with a simple smile. It makes you feel better and recharges the atmosphere around you. Others respond in an instant by smiling back.

Sing! Battered and beaten, Paul expressed joy through singing aloud in a prison. His joy penetrated heaven, and God sent an earthquake to free him. Coincidence? I believe that when we sing, the angels join in. The happiness we find in the Lord breaks down any and every invisible prison that has held us back.

Paul wrote, "Rejoice in the Lord always. Again I will say, rejoice" (Philippians 4:4) while in prison! He understood the strength of joy and therefore wasn't asking the church to rejoice. He commanded them. He had learned the secret of rejoicing *in* the trial, not afterward. His outright joy brought many souls into God's kingdom.

Anger releases negative chemical changes to the body. Laughter causes the opposite. Scientists Lee Berk and Stanley A. Tan of Loma Linda University (California) have determined that even the expectation of laughter, as a *positive* stress, benefits the immune system. Positive hormones, such as endorphins and neuromodulators, increase while the hormones related to negative stress, cortisol, and adrenaline, decrease.[18] Laughter serves as a protective valve that reduces extra tension.

> " Laughter restores the balance among all components of immune system. "

The immune system operates better with less tension. At the release of endorphins, the abdominal muscles tense up—releasing and ridding the body of toxins while aiding in digestion. Laughter restores the balance among all components of immune system.

Laughter actually speeds up the healing process. In some countries, laughter therapy replaces antidepressants or painkillers. It truly is the *best medicine.*

Norman Cousins, journalist and author, was diagnosed with a rare and fatal illness. Rejecting traditional medicine, he took massive doses of Vitamin C and watched comedy movies for hours every day. He discovered 10 minutes of deep belly laughs gave him two hours of pain free sleep. Eventually, he laughed himself to full recovery. Later, he wrote a book about how laughter had cured him, *Anatomy of an Illness: As Perceived by the Patient.*

Adults are said to laugh much less frequently than children, primarily because adults have less social interaction than do children. The more time we spend socializing, the more apt we are to laugh. In this matter, it would do us all well to be more like children: enjoy life and focus on finding good anywhere we can.

To sum up, we must learn to spend quality time with God in the inner sanctum of our hearts. Most people live in stressful environments and are bombarded with the constant sounds of traffic, radios, and television. When we retreat to that sanctuary where God speaks to our heart, he calms us and inspires us to move forward toward our destiny in him.

The word *inspiration* comes from the words *in spirit.* There was a time when inspiration was linked to God himself. To be inspired was to be in the Spirit. It was divine. God is always attempting to inspire us to a quality of life that is better than anything we have ever imagined. Sin is when we fail to grab the inspiration and enjoy the quality of life God is offering.

Follow the advice of Peter. "Make every effort to add to your faith goodness; and to goodness, knowledge; and to knowledge, self-control; and to self-control, perseverance; and to perseverance, godliness; and to godliness, mutual affection; and to mutual affection, love. He offers his own eight steps to a serene life: faith, virtue, knowledge, self-control, perseverance, godliness, brotherly kindness, love" (2 Peter 1:5–7). Before laying out these key developments, he admonishes the reader to *make every effort* to achieve these eight steps. This is how one achieves full Christian maturity.

Relaxing in God's presence helps with difficult decisions. Read the Bible. Listen to music that glorifies our savior. Ask for guidance and do not stop until you sense his peace. Learn to listen to and obey God's voice in your inner being as you dispel any thoughts that encourage fear or doubt.

THE REARVIEW MIRROR

Never be afraid to trust an
unknown future to a known God.
—Corrie ten Boom

One cannot move forward while constantly looking back. It is as impossible as driving a vehicle forward while constantly looking in the rearview mirror. We cannot change the past. Nonetheless, we have the power to change our attitude.

Even our very body teaches us to move forward, not backward. Our feet point forward. Our eyes see only what is in front of us. We must turn around to look behind. God's intention is that we always advance toward the goal.

The past is a great teacher but a terrible friend. Learn from it, but don't keep it hanging around. Perhaps you struggled with substance abuse. Or filed bankruptcy. Maybe a divorce taints your perception of your value.

God calls himself *God of Abraham, Isaac, and Jacob.* All these heroes of faith made mistakes. He is not God of perfect people. None exist. He is God of people like you and me. People who struggle through many challenges. Often we mess up; sometimes not.

Have you allowed those times to fester in your heart? Are you nursing hurts from someone who offended you? Camping out with past wounds only forms seeds of anger or bitterness that will destroy you, and even those around you.

None of us can change how the offender harmed us, but we must choose how we will handle it. God commands us to forgive. This is not an option. It is stated in both the Lord's Prayer and the verses directly following (Matthew 6:12, 14, 15).

As we ask God to extend grace to us by forgiving all our mistakes, so he commands that we show the same grace to others. Forgiveness does not negate the great wrong done to us. It simply liberates us from carrying the burden of the pain. Forgiveness frees our heart to live the abundant life promised by Jesus.

Release the one who harmed you to God. Let that person be God's problem, not yours. Take Paul's advice: Learn from the past, then forget it and move forward (Philippians 3:13–14).

Only through forgiveness can you experience harmony—in your family, within yourself, and with God. God wants to replace fear with peace, uncertainty with faith. He offers supernatural peace to grant our bodies, souls, and spirits divine rest.

7-Oliur, Unsplash

Pray with me:

> *God, I want to live the abundant life you promise all your followers. I want to experience the same intimacy as Moses, the same boldness as Abraham, and the same joy as Paul in any situation life throws at me. I want to live a victorious life filled with purpose and promise.*
>
> *I choose to forgive those who've harmed me, and I release all the pain they've caused me. I repent for holding on to it with unforgiveness in my heart. Nobody was ever more unfairly treated than Jesus, yet he prayed that you would forgive his killers.*
>
> *I release my past to you and now choose to press forward into the destiny you have planned for me. Amen.*

QUESTIONS FOR REFLECTION:

1. What are the warning signs in your life that you are getting angry?

2. How do you handle discouragement?

3. How do you handle anger?

4. How do you handle offense?

5. What can I change in my thinking to enjoy a happy and prosperous life?

Step 4

WORDS

Environment becomes Thoughts — Thoughts --→ Emotions — Emotions --→ **WORDS**

Words --→ Actions — Actions --→ Habits — Habits --→ Character

Character becomes your

DESTINY

"Nothing but trouble." My father shook his head. "Always misfortune follows me."

I heard those words from my earliest childhood. I could not understand them and wondered what my father meant by them.

"What do you mean, Father?" I asked one time. "What is misfortune, and why does it follow you?"

"What do you mean?" He looked at me in great surprise.

"Misfortune. You talk about it all the time. What does it mean, and why do you always have it?"

"Nothing, son." He shook his head. "I don't mean anything by it."

"Then, why do you always say it?"

"I don't know." He shrugged.

I intend no disrespect when I write about my father. He came from a different time and culture. He lived a hard life. What he never understood is that what we speak, we become. Such is the power of words.

If we choose to verbalize all our doubts, fears, and failures, all three will follow us, like hungry dogs, our entire lives. We control our future through our words. We use our brains and our hands in our careers, but our words determine our destiny.

WORDS ARE SUBSTANCE

Words have their own soul.
—Bertolt Brecht

Words run the world. Babies become aware of the meanings of some words around 7 months of age. Words surround us, mold us, guide us. Words permeate from birth to death. We live in a world of words.

The unseen, spiritual world exists in the same way. In fact, many scientists believe that everything we see can be divided into two invisible components: energy and information. Material objects contain energy. Everything—rocks, trees, human beings—vibrates and re-creates. Through this process they consume and release energy.

Information is the second component. Words are both energy and information. Words create and provide data. When a person tells you, I am a doctor, you receive a wealth of information from those four small words.

A doctor of biological studies, Peter P. Garyaev, established through testing that protein chromosomes contain all necessary information to form living organisms. He proved that every organism reacts to external influence. Those reactions cause changes in its DNA[19].

Dr. Masaru Emoto of Japan conducted extensive experiments on water[20]. He took water from the same source. To some glasses of water, he spoke words of blessing. The other glasses, he cursed. After a period of time, he froze the water from both and analyzed the crystals. Those from the blessing glass were exquisitely formed, like snowflakes. The cursed water took on the appearance of a clogged, filth-encrusted sewage pipe.

He did the same with music. The water exposed to classical or soothing music took on gorgeous shapes. The water exposed to heavy metal took on a sick brownish-yellow color. The crystals looked contorted and repulsive.

8- images http://www.masaru-emoto.net/english/water-crystal.html

One may scoff at such an experiment as immaterial to humans. However, our bodies consist of 70 to

> **Spoken words have the power to reshape my genetic code.**

80 percent water. Therefore, each spoken word influences every part of the body and brain. Those spoken by others or me affect bodily reaction so much, they have the ability to alter my health and how quickly I will age and could result in premature death.

Spoken words have the power to reshape my genetic code—not only mine, but for the next generations. Speak life into your family. Convey the message of possibilities. Spoken words give life or kill.

I. I. Belyavsky, a doctor of biological science, also wanted to understand the connection between words and the conscience of man. After extensive research, he arrived at two important conclusions: Every person is characterized by a specific spectrum of energy, and every word he hears brings energetic input. Words influence the genes. Affirming words have the power to extend health and life. Condemning words attract sickness, depression, and even death[21].

VITAL BUILDING BLOCKS

Words consist of a spiritual
chemical substance which exists forever.

Words vibrate with energy. Each contains a specific density in the spirit realm. As everything in the physical world—water, wind, plants, animals—is easily identifiable through our five senses, so are words in the unseen world. Although invisible to our senses, this sphere is more real because of its permanence. God created the visible by the invisible. Through words. Words don't simply exist in the moments they are spoken. Rather, their energy continues in the spirit realm. They consist of a spiritual chemical substance which exists forever. Past, present, and future continually exist together in the eternal perfect progressive tense. Every word we've spoken in our lifetime, we will hear again (Matt 12:36). Those words determine our eternal existence. Therefore, invisible words manifest into the seen. "By the word of the Lord the heavens were made, and all the host of them by the breath of His mouth" (Psalm 33:6 NKJV).

I think that a word is the most powerful weapon a person possesses. In the United States today, our hearts break as we witness the results of condemning, bullying words. Lost, desperate teens grab guns to annihilate others or kill themselves.

> ❝ Past, present, and future continually exist together in the eternal perfect progressive tense. ❞

Imagine the encouraging words spoken to Amy Purdy, who lost both legs and all kidney function from bacterial meningitis at age 19. Two years later, her father donated a kidney. Rather than wallow in her loss she states, "Instead of looking at our challenges and limitations as something negative or bad, we can begin to look at them as blessings, magnificent gifts that can be used to ignite our imaginations and help us go further than we ever knew we could go.[22]"

Purdy competed in the Paralympics and took home a bronze medal for snowboarding. Later, she competed on Dancing with the Stars and came in second place. Never underestimate the power of words to build up or tear down. One could argue that they are the greatest power on earth.

The book of James warns us about not controlling our tongue (James 3:2–6). He warns that the tongue controls the entire body. What we speak, we become. He also compares careless or angry words to a raging forest fire. It has the power to defile the whole person and destroy those around us.

My students and I once had a discussion about how much our tongues affect our entire lives. We concluded that it's like an on/off switch between the head and heart—between the centers of reasoning and emotions.

In a fit of temper, our tongues explode with angry verbiage, never allowing our brain the opportunity to think through the consequences of them. Or, we may use words to manipulate others to our way of thinking without taking their wishes or feelings into consideration. In the first instance, the heart rules through rage. In the second, the mind controls the words without consulting the heart. The mature person understands how to keep both in harmonious balance.

COMMANDING WORDS

Say something, not because you should be saying something.
Say something when you have something to say.
—Richard Votly

Jesus chose his words with great wisdom and authority. We easily see how he used them in his everyday life and his ministry. He rebuked a storm and ordered peace (Mark 4:39). He ordered life to the dead (Mark 5:41). He commanded demons to leave people (Mark 1:25).

Through words, he healed the sick. A Roman officer begged Jesus, "Speak a word, and my servant will be healed" (Matthew 8:8 NKJV). He understood the power of the spoken word. Everything he did was through the power of his *words*.

One could argue that Jesus had such success with words because he was God's son. However, we know of men in the Old Testament who spoke to nature and it obeyed. Elijah, every bit as human as any of us, commanded the clouds to withhold rain. After three and a half years of drought, he spoke again, and they obeyed, saturating the earth with life-sustaining rain (1 Kings 17–18; James 5:17–18).

Joshua ordered the sun to stand still during a crucial battle. It *happened* (Joshua 10:12–14). Many have debated about what really took place that day. Scientists put forward hypotheses while theologians make statements. Neither matters here. The fact is that Joshua spoke to the sun and it obeyed.

Are you ready to speak to nature in the same manner and expect results? Why or why not? The same God who commanded Moses to talk to a rock guides us today. He longs to show the same power through *us* as them.

> ❝ Everything Jesus did was through the power of his words. ❞

Again, *watch your words*. King Solomon warns, "A man's stomach shall be satisfied from the fruit of his mouth" (Proverbs 18:20 NKJV). As the food we eat affects our physical bodies, so the words we speak determine our destiny. No amount of healthy eating will counter the effect of the words used to feed our mind, soul, and spirit.

I read an article in which a 3-year-old reportedly sang to his unborn sister. However, she developed complications at birth and was placed in the NICU unit. As her condition worsened, the mother took him in to see her. As he gazed on the wee infant, he began singing his favorite song, "You are my sunshine, my only sunshine. You make me happy when skies are gray." Almost immediately, she responded. The nurse asked the boy to continue. "You are the only sunshine I have. Please don't take my sunshine away." The baby's breathing improved, and shortly after that, the doctors released her to go home.[23]

WORD PACKAGES

There are words - like wounds, words - like a court,
With them, people do not surrender and do not take prisoners.
You can kill with a word, you can save with a word.
With a word, you can take armies to follow you.
With a word, you can sell, and betray, and buy.
A word can be transformed into a smashing lead.
—*Vadim Shefner*

Imagine words like packages. The weight of them determines the heaviness of the package, perhaps indicating its contents. A single word changes weight by the emotion in which it is uttered. *Yes, dear* spoken in anger carries a negative heaviness over the *Yes, dear* of joy.

Our soul consists of three parts: feelings, mind, and will. These parts of our inner being directly influence the weight of our spoken words. Words of peace, faith, and love bring lightness to the hearer. In the unseen world, those words come from the transformed mind, a mind changed by dwelling in God's presence and reading his Word.

When we bow to God's will, everything we utter follows. We speak words of life because he is life. We speak words of hope because he is hope. We declare words of destiny because he is our destiny. Our very words can carry the weight of God's glory.

Science also teaches us that words vibrate in space, known as electromagnetic oscillation. Each sound carries its own energy code, charge, and unique image. Once paired with emotion, spoken words release energy that emits life or death. The stronger the emotion, the greater the charge.

As Dr. Emoto proved in his water experiments, every vibration carries the power of life or destruction. This is why King Solomon issued his warning. "Death and life are in the power of the tongue, and those who love it will eat its fruit" (Proverbs 18:21 NKJV).

> ❝ Each word carries its own energy code, charge, and unique image. Once paired with emotion, spoken words release energy that emits life or death. ❞

Angels carry our spoken words into God's throne room. "Then another angel, having a golden censer, came and stood at the altar. He was given much incense, that he should offer it with the prayers of all the saints upon the golden altar which was before the throne. And the smoke of the incense, with the prayers of the saints, ascended before God from the angel's hand" (Revelation 8: 3–4 NLV).

Angels take our prayers (unseen, human substance) and mix them with (visible, divine) incense. Afterwards, they offer all up to God. The smoke of the incense moves him to answer them.

The word, as a living organism, has its own structure spirit. By merging the visible with the invisible worlds, we come to understand that words *are* matter.

WORDS HEAL

Thou weighest thy words before thou givest them breath.
—*William Shakespeare, Othello*

Longevity, happiness, and the words we speak are connected. "If you want to enjoy life and see many happy days, keep your tongue from speaking evil and your lips from telling lies" (1 Peter 3:10 NLT). Pleasant words motivate us to do our best. King Solomon compares such words as medicinal.

"Gracious words are a honeycomb, sweet to the soul and healing to the bones" (Proverbs 16:24 NIV). Positive words inspire us. Not only that, they contribute to good health.

The American Association of Psychotherapists released findings in which the health of persons of faith and atheists was compared and documented. They concluded that, on average, people who regularly attend church and pray live longer than those who reject religion. They also enjoy a higher percentage of health against such diseases as cancer, hypertension, and diabetes. Coincidence? Not at all. Prayer is filled with positive words that comfort the soul and inspire faith.

Russian scientists have come to the same conclusion. Verbal information influences a person's entire immune system. Medical personnel used positive, kind words during their psychotherapist sessions and recorded the results. They found that, not only did such language lighten the spirits of their patients, it also changed their blood count. It raised its energy capacity and cell immunity. The DNA structure changed to enable faster healing. Through specific word therapy, patients recovered five to seven days faster than those who took medications only. They also found that such words as love, hope, faith, and kindness influenced the people most.[24]

Words also influence your nation. "By the blessing of the upright the city is exalted, but it is overthrown by the mouth of the wicked" (Proverbs 11:11). Righteous people release words of blessing that influence their world. Wicked people spew evil that destroys both people and the nation.

> ❝ Scientific studies have proven that verbal information influences a person's entire immune system. ❞

Right words release life and energy into the atmosphere, which affects our environment. Learn to refrain from *all* harsh words. "Bite your tongue," our grandparents admonished us. Be diligent to speak blessings into your family and friends, not disabling curses.

How is it possible to continually speak gentle, affirming words in a world of turmoil? By remembering to place not only our body, soul, and spirit under our Creator's control, but also the tongue.

A young man once confessed to a wise person he respected that he had spoken falsehoods about him.

"I'm very sorry for what I said," the young man confessed. "Please forgive me."

"Of course, I forgive you," the wise man answered. "However, I'd like you to do something for me."

"Anything!" The young man was eager to show how repentant he truly was.

"Good." The older man smiled. "I want you to go home, take a feather pillow up on the roof of your house, and tear it open. After the wind has scattered every feather, come back and see me."

"Of course." He returned a short while later.

"I've done what you asked. Now what do you want me to do?"

"I want you to go back and gather up every feather."

"But, that's impossible," the young man exclaimed. "I could never find them all. The wind blew them all over town."

"Exactly." The wise man's smile remained gentle. "So are the words that we allow to fly out of our mouths. We can never collect them again."

The young man looked stricken.

"Son, I trust you will watch every word that you speak from now on."[25]

9- Ilyass Seddoug, Unsplash

KILLING CURSES

The reality of blessings and curses coming from the same source—our mouth—should sober us. Jacob unknowingly cursed his favorite wife, Rachel, as he moved his family back to Canaan. His father-in-law accused him of stealing the family gods (Genesis 31).

Jacob scoffed and told him if anyone among his people had taken them, that person would die. Rachel had hidden them. She didn't die at that moment but years later in childbirth. The strength of the spoken word caused her death.

The story teaches us that words build up or destroy, especially when spoken by the leader, be it the home, church, or workplace. Also, those dabbling in the occult open spiritual doors for the enemy to penetrate. That practice hinders God's protection.

A more modern example of the power of spoken curses comes through a married couple. The wife was a terrible cook.

"I'm sick of this slop," her husband screamed at every meal. "You will never learn how to cook."

The marriage failed, and the couple divorced. The wife became successful in every other area of her life, but never learned to cook. Her ex-husband's words haunted her all her life. He in turn suffered indigestion issues, and no doctor could discover the reason for it.

Often, we curse ourselves without realizing it. Have you ever said, "He drives me crazy" about your child? Or "My grandpa died of colon cancer; maybe I'll get it too." Or "Everyone divorces in my family. It's just a matter of time before my own marriage falls apart."

We speak death into our futures without knowing we caused it. Instead of remarking, See, I told you so, we need to repent of all self-inflicted curses, many of which burst from disappointment or conflict.

A teenage girl struggles with the pimples on her face. Every morning she spends hours in front of the mirror trying to cover up all her skin imperfections. Her father waits for her in order to drive her to school, and he is frustrated with her being late. Once she came even later than usual. He spilled out all that he was irritated about. "You are wasting your time in front of that mirror. You'll never get rid of those zits," he roared. Twenty years later, already raising a few children, she is still fighting pimples.

A few times in the Bible, God himself shut up people's mouths. When God is planning to do something and he is working with people who can intervene or even destroy his plan, God will close their mouth, so people will not change God's will by their own mouth. It happened when God was planning to bring John the Baptist before Jesus and the angel appeared to Zacharias and said that. Zacharias didn't believe (Luke 1:18). That's why God made him silent and not able to speak until the child was born. This is a universal law; whatever we say will be fulfilled in some kind of form. God created that law and he is following the law too. That's why he knew that Zacharias could mess up God's plan with his words. God didn't have any other way but just to shut him up.

Also, when God told the Israelites to go into the Promised Land and conquer the first city, Jericho, he told them to be silent for six days. God knew that it was something new for them and they had never experienced the victory; that was why they didn't have faith. In their unbelief, they could have said negative things. They might have started complaining.

Complaining is a very dangerous form of meditation. In meditation we think about something until we produce the associated emotions, which reinforces it as real or absolute. When people complain, they remind themselves of negative past or present events and magnify a problem until it gets larger. Those negative words will steal their faith and they will not produce spiritual energy for angels to use to take down those walls. Negative words and a negative spirit are contagious and very dangerous because it starts destructive mechanisms according to the spiritual law. God is bound by this law, despite the fact that he himself created it.

TYPES OF CURSES

Words generally are the avenue through which blessings or curses are released. Blessings activate positive changes in a person's life. Curses stump growth or destroy. Each is the alternate side of one coin. Where one can be blessed, one can also be cursed.

Many people live under generational curses, yet are unaware of it. They fail to understand how they cannot succeed in certain areas of their lives. Sometimes, studying one's history helps to understand.

Satan uses seemingly harmless activities, such as voodoo or playing the Ouija board to destroy destiny. Take the subject of curses seriously to ensure that the enemy does not destroy yours. Understand that there are many types of curses:

- Generational: when a parent, grandparent, or other ancestor did something that opened the door for a curse. The Bible says that some curses can go back four generations.

- Self-acquired: through a person's own actions, such as stealing, lying, disobedience, playing demonic-influenced video games.

- Induced: proclaiming a curse over another person, especially in a thoughtless rage.

- Self-proclaimed: constant proclamation of negative words over oneself.

What might be some possible indicators that someone is living under a curse?

- Inherited family illness (Deuteronomy 28:21)

- Chronic illness (Deuteronomy 28:27)

- Emotional instability (Deuteronomy 28:28)

- Rebellion (2 Kings 9:30–34)

- Infertility (Deuteronomy 28:18)

- Divorce (Deuteronomy 28:30)

- Poverty or financial hardship (Deuteronomy 28:17, 47–48)

- Frequent accidents and/or premature death (Deuteronomy 28:29)

- Loss of identity (Deuteronomy 28:43–44)

Jesus offers full deliverance from any curse and its consequence. We only need to truly repent and renounce every known curse, claiming the power of his blood. I have prayed for Jesus to remove every curse in my life and those in my family. I have prayed for many others in my years of ministry, and their lives have changed completely. The good news is that we can break any curse today in Jesus's name.

If you feel as if an invisible barrier stands between you and all God offers, go to his throne room and ask him to show you what it is. Expect to receive his mercy and grace, knowing his eternal love for you. Cry out to the one who created you and loves you.

Pray in this manner:

> *Heavenly Father, I come to you through your son, Jesus Christ. I repent and ask forgiveness for all my sins. I believe that the sacrifice of Jesus Christ gives me authority to destroy every negative word and curse spoken against me.*

> *I reject Satan and all his lies, and I forbid him to rule in my life (and in the lives of my spouse and children). I ask You, Lord, to completely destroy any influence that Satan has had in my life. In the name of Jesus, break every curse or generational sin that may have been passed on to me through my family bloodline.*

> *I also confess and reject every word that I have spoken about myself or my spouse, parents, relatives, or friends. Let every negative word or curse spoken against me, my family, or my future be annulled and demolished in the spirit realm.*

> *I claim the blood of Jesus Christ to destroy every sin and factor that prevents me from moving forward to live an abundant life. In the name of Jesus Christ, let all the shackles be destroyed—any burden, any generational sin and curse. I receive forgiveness, freedom, and mercy to live a new life in Christ. Amen.*

RELEASING BLESSING

In prayer, it is better to have a heart without words
than the words without a heart.
—Mahatma Gandhi

By blessing others, we become blessed. Joy, peace, and life spread through our own beings as we release the blessing to others. In other words, we partake of the same blessing we give away.

Publicly encourage your children. God did. He stated, "This is my Son, whom I love; with him I am well pleased" (Matthew 3:17 NIV). In that statement, God recognizes Jesus as his own son, confesses his love for him, and announces his support. Can we do less with our own children?

Children who receive no affirmation at home will seek it elsewhere. Fathers, compliment your daughters. Otherwise they may satisfy this need in the arms of an unscrupulous man. Mothers, encourage your sons to grow into strong, protective men, not the helpless wimps that society tries to make of males.

Fathers blessing their offspring is an ancient tradition, one worth practicing today. Set aside a day to release blessing over your entire family and celebrate it as a turning point in the family dynamic. Let them know that you are now committed to speaking only words of life over them and will work hard not to speak any more words of negativity. Stay accountable to them by keeping your promise to bless and never curse again.

We may love our spouse and children but how often do we express it through the power of words? Tell your spouse of your love and support. Tell your children you are proud of them for working hard.

Express, through words, your appreciation to your church family, your friends, your coworkers, and the checkout clerk at the grocery store. Spread the blessing, and it will come back to you.

Bless, do not curse, a difficult boss. Leave challenging people in God's hands because only he is qualified to deal with them. Only he knows their hearts and life struggles.

It is human nature to want to curse our enemies—especially those who hate us and wish us harm. Sometimes we forget God loves them as much as us. We must bless our enemies because Jesus commanded it (Luke 6:28).

Remember, we walk before God. We will answer to him for what we do. Let God deal with the others. As Jesus told Peter, "Whatever happens to John is not your issue. You follow me" (John 21:22, paraphrased).

The most important person to bless is our Creator. David admonished, "Bless the Lord, O my soul; And all that is within me, bless His holy name! Bless the Lord, O my soul, and forget not all His benefits: Who forgives all your iniquities, Who heals all your diseases, Who redeems your life from destruction, Who crowns you with lovingkindness and tender mercies, Who satisfies your mouth with good things, So that your youth is renewed like the eagle's" (Psalm 103:1–5 NKJV).

Does the Almighty God need our blessing? No, but by blessing him, we establish a channel through which blessings flow into our lives from heaven. *All* God offers us—wisdom, joy, strength, mercy, forgiveness—becomes ours when we bless *him*. Bless God, even in difficult circumstances.

Blessing God renews us, physically, mentally, emotionally, and spiritually. Blessing him removes the urge to complain, facilitates contentment, and brings us closer to destiny.

10- Priscills Du Preez, Unsplash

ENLARGE MY TERRITORY

*The greater the humility with which
we kneel before the Lord,
The more He pours out his blessings.*

—Unknown

Some people truly have nobody to speak blessing into their lives. Either their home environment is so negative they hear only curses, or they find themselves in a spiritual vacuum. What can they do?

Many people in the Bible carried names with meaning. Abraham means *Father of multitudes.* Moses means *Drawn from the water.* Jabez, mentioned in 1 Chronicles 4:9–10, means *One who brings grief.*

What mother would give her son such a name? Was he unwanted? Did she endure a difficult delivery? The Bible does not explain the source of her pain. Every time his mother called him home for dinner or his friends yelled out in play, he heard, *One who brings grief, can you come out and play ball?* Or *One who brings grief, be quiet and listen to your teacher.* He could never escape his name. Every time someone uttered it, it served as a word curse in his life.

What could he do? Somewhere in his life experience, Jabez cried out to God. He prayed, "Oh, that you would bless me indeed, and enlarge my territory, that your hand would be with me, and that you would keep me from evil, that I may not cause pain" (1 Chronicles 4:10 NKJV).

He sought to reverse the curse his mother had laid on his life. What was God's response? "So, God granted him what he requested" (1 Chronicles 4:10). He killed the curse.

Jabez became more famous than all his brothers and gained the respect of his tribe. All this happened because he turned to God rather than allowing bitterness or hopelessness settle in his heart.

Any one of us can do the same. God has mercy for all. He has a special plan for every life. Not only does he have the power to change your identity and destiny, he *longs* to do it. Below are only a few verses that show his true heart toward us.

> "Blessed be the God and Father of our Lord Jesus Christ, who has blessed us with every spiritual blessing in the heavenly places in Christ" (Ephesians 1:3 NKJV).

> "As His divine power has given to us all things that pertain to life and godliness, through the knowledge of Him who called us by glory and virtue" (2 Peter 1:3 NKJV).

"But you are God, ready to pardon, gracious and merciful, slow to anger, abundant in kindness, and did not forsake them" (Nehemiah 9:17 NKJV).

"Blessed be the God and Father of our Lord Jesus Christ, who has blessed us with every spiritual blessing in the heavenly places in Christ" (Ephesians 1:3 NKJV).

"As His divine power has given to us all things that pertain to life and godliness, through the knowledge of Him who called us by glory and virtue" (2 Peter 1:3 NKJV).

"But you are God, ready to pardon, gracious and merciful, slow to anger, abundant in kindness, and did not forsake them" (Nehemiah 9:17 NKJV).

"And my God shall supply all your need according to His riches in glory by Christ Jesus" (Philippians 4:19 NKJV).

"Now to him who is able to do exceedingly abundantly above all that we ask or think" (Ephesians 3:20 NKJV).

"The blessing of the Lord makes one rich, and he adds no sorrow with it" (Proverbs 10:22 NKJV).

"The Lord makes poor and makes rich; he brings low and lifts up" (1 Samuel 2:7 NKJV).

"This Book of the Law shall not depart from your mouth, but you shall meditate in it day and night, that you may observe to do according to all that is written in it. For then you will make your way prosperous, and then you will have good success" (Joshua 1:8 NKJV).

THE ETERNAL WORD

Prayer is a key that reveals the Word of God to us.
It also opens our eyes and hearts to the Spirit of God.
—Unknown

God created with words. He spoke, it happened (Genesis 1). Compare that to John's account: "In the beginning was the Word, and the Word was with God, and the Word was God. He was in the beginning with God. All things were made through Him, and without Him nothing was made that was made. In Him was life, and the life was the light of men. ... And the Word became flesh and dwelt among us, and we beheld His glory, the glory as of the only begotten of the Father, full of grace and truth" (John 1:1–4; 14).

When Jesus walked on earth, he breathed life in words also. He set people free. He healed the sick. He gave the down-trodden hope.

> The more we meditate on God and his Word, the more perfectly we will experience his will in our lives.

Today, we keep in tune with God's heart through prayer, worship, and reading the Bible. It is far more than a book of historical records and teachings. God's Word gives life because it contains life. When facing difficult decisions, pray first. Acknowledge your own helplessness. Wait to hear God's response.

Sometimes he speaks directly in your heart. Other times, he uses the Bible. As you read, a phrase or concept will quicken the spirit within you. Then you will know it is his answer to you. It happened to me so many times. I love my Bible because God uses it to speak to me. I have so many side notes in my Bible. Learn how to work with the book, and it will guide you. Memorize verses to store their truth deep in your heart.

God promised success to Joshua if he would remain faithful to Moses's teachings (Joshua 1:8). He revealed to King David the importance of hanging out with the right people (Psalm 1:1–3). The more we meditate on God and keep reading his Word, the more perfectly we will experience his will in our lives.

Meditate. This is a biblical as well as a psychological process that makes the unseen, seen. Ponder God's love for you. Think on his august power. Let those thoughts sink so deep into your soul that you never doubt their veracity again.

Write your thoughts. Affirm what you know to be true about God on paper. Write out what you believe are his plans for you. Journal your prayers, goals, and hopes. Read books about others who changed their destinies and discuss them with others.

Pray the following to release blessings in your life, your family, your church, and your world:

> *Father, in the name of Jesus, I thank you that I can come to you in utter confidence. I know that you hear me and will answer. I confess that the Word of God is near me, in my mouth and in my heart. Today I choose life. Today I receive every blessing you offer. You have given me the keys to the kingdom so that whatever I bind on earth is bound in heaven. Whatever I loose on earth is loosed in heaven.*

> *I release blessing where there have been curses. I release life against all death. I release peace and unity against all strife and division. I proclaim soundness where there has been confusion. I confess that the Word of God says to decree a thing and it shall be established.*

> *Today I prophesy blessing over my life, blessing devoid of sorrow. I confess that the blessing of the Lord brings prosperity and joy. I declare that life-giving wisdom flows from my deepest being. I release health against all sickness. I pursue peace with my God. I speak peace into all the people who surround me. I declare all in the name of Jesus.*

QUESTIONS FOR REFLECTION:

1. If you realized that every word becomes matter, what would you say?

2. What words would you stop saying?

3. What will be your confession from this day forward?

Step 5

ACTIONS

> Environment becomes Thoughts — Thoughts --→ Emotions — Emotions --→ Words
> Words --→ **ACTIONS** — Actions --→ Habits — Habits --→ Character
> Character becomes your
> DESTINY

THE PRIORITY WHEEL

Thought without action is waste of time.
—Unknown

What do I want to do with my life?

I pondered that question during my freshman year of college. When we are young, we often find it difficult to think seriously about our future. However, that is what I did. I decided for the first time in my life to write down what was important to me and set goals.

Some took longer than the time frame I had allowed myself, which discouraged me. However, instead of thinking of it as a personal failure, I forgave myself and moved on. Every year I revisit my set goals in order to realize how much I have accomplished through walking with God. After analyzing each one to measure my growth, I establish new goals for the coming year. By keeping my priorities lined up in his order, God remains faithful to help me achieve each one.

Goals propel one into action, and action often starts with words. The first four chapters of this book covered our external environment that conditions the internal spheres of thought, emotion, and words. We learned the value of the spoken word in the last chapter.

Verbalize what you wish to achieve. Write it down. Realize that partnering your desires to God's will takes you where you want to go.

Some people spend years learning about how to set goals, yet never act on that knowledge. Others act without a plan. Neither brings success. Moreover, do not equate busyness with action. If you immerse yourself so deeply into business to provide for your family's physical comforts, you could end up neglecting their spiritual *needs*.

Or, perhaps you devote so much time on improving your physical health that you fail to cultivate your mind or spirit. In ei-

> ❝ People who fail to act on their dreams turn into old people filled with regret. ❞

ther situation, the family suffers from your lack of balance. Balancing the information you receive from this book with proper action is like a bird with two wings. It takes both wings in equal balance to achieve the flight to destiny.

Remember that people who fail to *act* on their dreams turn into old people filled with regret, so let us begin the process by prioritizing your goals in the proper order.

Throughout my life, I have set goals in six areas. I call this my priority wheel. I find I live a fulfilled life as long as I concentrate on these six main points. The following are how I divide these goals:

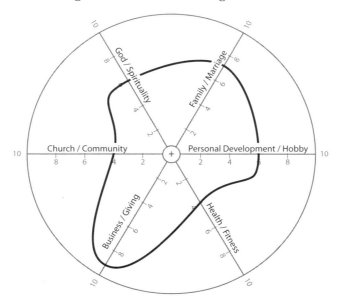

1. God / Spirituality

2. Family / Marriage

3. Church / Community

4. Business / Giving

5. Health / Fitness

6. Personal Development / Hobby

There are six spokes in my illustration. Each one represents a specific area of life. For any wheel to turn properly, the spokes must be of *even* length. As you study the wheel, ask yourself, *How fulfilled am I at this stage of my life? Do I live with purpose and a smoothness throughout each day, or is the ride bumpy and off balance?*

Take a few minutes to evaluate each of these six points before moving on to read the rest of this chapter.

PRIORITY #1 – GOD

A person needs to die just once and
their priorities will change immediately.
—Unknown

The wife of a billionaire asked her house servants to bring her favorite dress to her as she lay on her deathbed. Soon after the garment arrived, pain overtook her. She clutched the edge of the dress in her agony and died with it in her grasp. As the mortician set about to prepare her body for burial, he found he could not unclench the fingers of the dead woman. He was forced to snip as much of the cloth from around her hand as possible, leaving a small scrap forever in her clasp[26].

Her dying request seems to illustrate what mattered most to her in her lifetime—a treasured possession. What controls us, owns us. God tells us that what we value in the unseen, we can take beyond the grave. He assures us that if we seek his kingdom, his purposes, he will provide for the temporal needs we have today (Matthew 6:33). Everything else lines up when we keep God first.

God's kingdom is not an abstract. It is a real dimension with its own set

> Everything in life lines up when we keep God first.

of laws that exists beyond our natural realm. When we choose to dwell in this kingdom, we access the supernatural atmosphere he offers and experience a deep peace incomprehensible to nonbelievers. God's divine peace overrides the harshest of human circumstances to keep our hearts anchored in him.

Earthly law tells us to take whatever we want from life, live for the present, and achieve our goals at any price. God's kingdom tells us to live for him first, others second, and ourselves last. Only our love for God helps us give up that mindset to live with the same humility Jesus modeled on earth.

Fretting over our daily needs wastes time and energy because Jesus also promised his followers that he would attend to those needs, as long as they pursued his kingdom first. Nourishing the body comes second to feeding the soul. The body ages and dies, but the soul lives forever. The body remains limited to time on earth. The soul moves on to eternity.

What made King David successful in life? David understood this principle of serving God's kingdom first. He wrote, *"One thing I have desired of the Lord, that will I seek: That I may dwell in the house of the Lord all the days of my life, To behold the beauty of the Lord, And to inquire in His temple"* (Psalm 27:4 NKJV, emphasis added).

David kept his priorities aligned with God. He knew everything he possessed came from God. Every blessing from heaven flowed from the proper order in his life.

God had Samuel anoint David as the king after Saul because God knew David's *heart*. David relied on God for every victory. He soaked in God's presence. He knew God as an intimate friend. The groundwork for leading a nation came from the fields where David led sheep.

Although David stumbled numerous times in his lifetime, he *always* returned to God. His triumphs, doubts, failures, and exhilaration have ministered to countless people for more than 3000 years. Such is the influence of the person who puts God *first*.

PRIORITY # 2 – FAMILY

The absence of a dream ruins people.
—John F. Kennedy

A man watched his place of business burn down, went home, and slumped at the table.

"Daddy, why are you crying?" his little daughter asked.

"Baby, I lost everything," he sobbed. "Everything"

"But, Daddy." She laid a hand on his knee and looked into his face. "How can you say that? Don't you still have me? And Mommy? And God?"

We already discussed the need to make God our first priority in life. Family comes second. Our present society degrades the value of family in many ways. Males are bashed on TV with cute commercials and sitcoms where children appear so much more clever. Divorce and affairs are treated with a simple explanation of falling out of love or people changing.

According to statistics, fewer than 50 percent of American children grow up with the original family intact. Many are raised with one parent, usually the mother, and homosexual parents are on the rise.

Our society is in serious need of recovery. It will happen only through the reinstitution of family as God intended—a man and

> **As husband and wife love, honor and serve God first, the stronger the bond grows between them.**

woman who fear the Lord and raise their children with strong morals.

The true followers of Jesus need to step up and model God's order for the rest of society, starting in their own neighborhood. Couples who respect and honor one another and control through loving discipline catch the attention of a struggling, bewildered society. They may scoff at first but cannot ignore the fruit of a family living in harmony.

Joshua stated that his entire household intended to serve the Lord (Joshua 24:15). This is the only path to true success. As husband and wife love, honor, and serve God first, the stronger the bond grows between *them*. The strength of that commitment further blesses their children's stability and security.

As each of us yields to God, he transforms our character by teaching us understanding, patience, and unconditional love. It is the responsibility of each generation to develop through God's leading and pass what we've learned on to the next generation. We are to teach our children truth, thus giving them a legacy that they may pass on to their own children.

Society has blurred the roles of men, women, and children to the point that we see the results in the belittling of males, battering of women, sex trafficking, and gender confusion among children.

God created man to lead the family. He is not to be a dictator. He is to lead with the same love Christ had for the church—to die for his family if necessary. As the priest of the home, the man is responsible for blessing both his wife and his children. He is the family intercessor. Just as the Jewish priest stood before God and pleaded for mercy on behalf of the nation, so the father must assume this crucial role of offering sincere prayer for his wife and children.

He must model, through his behavior, how he cherishes his wife, listens to her, and supports her emotionally as well as financially. In this way, his sons and daughters understand the male role as they enter adulthood.

The wife is to submit to her husband's authority (Ephesians 5:22). Many people, including believers in Jesus, misunderstand this commandment. They think it means subservience. Not so! The Bible clearly states that God created male and female equal (Genesis 1:27). He made both in his image.

Charging the man with the responsibility of leading the home avoids confusion. In a corporation or on any sports team, many offer input, but a single person makes the final decision. It is the same within the family. A wise man listens to his wife before making that final decision. Yes, God calls for the woman to submit to her husband, but he commands the man to love his wife with the same intensity and willingness to *die* for her.

The key to this concept is *respect*. The husband respects his wife as his equal. She respects him as the leader of the home. The result is harmony among them and their children. Your first priority after God is your spouse, not your job, children, or hobbies.

Paul instructs the children to obey their parents, echoing one of the original Ten Commandments. The children's respect launches the mechanism of blessing into their own lives, which God promises will be long and prosperous.

God places a high premium on honor. People of honor respect all humankind, old and young, rich and poor, those in authority, and those they lead. Instill this principle in your children to avoid hardships in their own lives later. Honor releases all kinds of blessings, health, financial and spiritual prosperity.

When all members of the family honor God's authority first, along with the proper order in the home—the father as leader, the mother respecting his position, and the children honoring both—joy fills the home. Others witness the harmony and long for the same. Family by family, we can rebuild a strong and healthy society.

12- http://www.joinedwithjesus.org/parents

PRIORITY #3 – CHURCH

Only a burning church brings light.
—Buenaventura Durruti

A vibrant, thriving church grows on the foundation of strong families. The order in the home carries over into the local body of Christ. A healthy church nourishes the soul as food feeds the body.

God created us to live in community. The elder lead the younger through example. They model the proper way for husbands to cherish their wives and train their children to do the same. We also need the church to maintain spiritual balance in our lives.

Attending church and actively engaging with the body of Christ are two different factors. Attendance may make you feel good, like watching a lively game of basketball. However, unless you get on the court and grab the ball, you remain a spectator. True discipleship is not a spectator sport. It's a serious conflict with the dark forces of hell.

The body of Christ—the *ekklesia* in Greek, meaning a congregation of members—is the visible representation of the resurrected Christ. He sits at God's right hand while the Holy Spirit leads us into battle that brings victory for all and glory to God. As such, he has given each believer specific skills and talents for us to work *together* to accomplish his will.

> ❝ True discipleship is not a spectator sport. ❞

This *ekklesia* is the mystery that God kept hidden until after Jesus came to earth. If Jesus granted tremendous power to his followers (Matthew 16:18–19), then why do so many Christians live defeated lives? I believe it is because many believers do not understand the revelation of the true church's power and function. As a member of this *ekklesia*, every one of us has power to stand against all the evil forces of darkness. *In Christ*, we are stronger than any demon because *he* is the head of the church.

We can only experience the power when we embrace this mystery. We are Christ's body on earth. It's easy to say it, but you need to have an experience with God in which God himself, through the Holy Spirit, will open the truth to you. Our authority extends beyond life here. In eternity, we will judge the angels (1 Corinthians 6:3) because of the authority and position given to us by God. Once the church embraces this revelation and unifies, she becomes *unstoppable*.

Another deterrent to living in the fullness of our purpose is becoming overly occupied with our physical lives and neglecting the spiritual realm God called us to. He confronted the Jews over this in the book of Haggai. He accused them of spending all their time tending to their homes while neglecting *his* house. The prophet informed the Jews of the direct connection between honoring God's house and their prosperity. He promised to blow away the works of their hands as long as they ignored his place where they were to worship him (Haggai 1:4, 8–9).

A simple act of moving chairs in your local church or greeting people at the door can open windows of blessing in your life. God is moved by people with servant hearts. He can cause you to get a promotion you have long desired, or bring new business contracts across your desk. God expects us to honor what is important to Him first. *Then* we can expect his blessings to flow to us.

PRIORITY #4 – WORK

*A successful business always starts
with a big idea, not big money.*

A reporter for the well-known *Forbes* magazine surveyed a group of millionaires to learn the secrets of their success. Most agreed that the first secret was they were *not afraid of failure.* Every one of the surveyed persons admitted to failing in their business decisions at least one time. They chose to learn from their mistakes and move on.

The second secret was they *never settled* once they'd achieved success. Instead, they evaluated their past accomplishments and strove for more. Through creative solutions to difficult problems, they enjoyed the satisfaction of overcoming every obstacle. More income followed each success.

Most agreed the third factor to their success lay in *successful marriage.* They understood the importance of having a spouse that supported them through the highs and lows of life.[27] Spouse and family influenced their decisions and helped keep them focused.

Successful people know how to prioritize and act on it because they have *vision.* Vision is the ability to see beyond one's current circumstances. That mental picture or business idea is what keeps you moving forward when all you can see is dead ends.

A God-given vision connects you to greater possibilities. It mobilizes every part of your being, renews your faith, and keeps you from quitting.

The Bible says that without vision people perish (Proverbs 29:18 KJV). In other words, life is wasted without it. Vision motivates successful people to strategize.

Strategy births the necessary energy to push forward to achieve. The passion in vision-driven people propels them on their journey toward destiny, like feeding coal to a steam engine. The hotter the fire, the faster the pace. Passion is contagious energy that not only keeps us active but also fires up those around us.

Embrace and understand these three words: *vision, strategy, and passion*. They will change your outlook on life. A good, God-inspired vision, backed by strategic planning and energized by pure passion, catapults you into the divine purpose for which you were born.

But what if you are stuck in a job you don't like in this current period of your life? Set time aside to develop the necessary skills to change your occupation. Read. Take classes. Find opportunities to develop your own talents. God implanted unique gifts in each one of us. Discover yours and develop it.

You already have what you need! God always takes what we have, the natural of our lives, and joins it to his power to make the result supernatural. Jesus took five loaves of bread, prepared and baked by human hands, and transformed them into meals for over 5000 people. Jesus took water, fetched by human servants, and transformed it to wine. God chooses to use his creatures to move in supernatural ways.

However, many people get stuck just because they think they need to get something that they do not possess in that moment. The reality is that God has already placed in and around us *everything* that we need to accomplish his purposes for our life. Skills, talents, people around us—all serve to connect to his infinite knowledge.

Use it all and you will be blessed because God *wants* to use *you* to accomplish miraculous things for his kingdom.

God wants you to experience *prosperity with purpose,* to bring the Kingdom of God in every sphere of our lives. God cannot bless us until we honor his way first. With the money we earn, we need to adhere to the principle of the first fruits (Proverbs 3:9–10) and tithing.

Tithing is a physical expression that we have chosen to put God first in our financial, home, and spiritual life. God has promised to "rebuke the devourer" (Malachi 3:11 NKJV) when we tithe. The devourer is anything hindering your success.

Tithing is a covenant action between God and yourself. It connects you to the same supernatural power that he promised Abraham. Abraham supernaturally became the father of many nations and experienced prosperity because he was a man of faith who always tithed. God promises the same to you. Give to him first and prepare to live an extraordinary life.

PRIORITY # 5—HEALTH

The absence of a dream ruins people.
—*John F. Kennedy*

Recently, I visited a gentleman who had worked hard for the last 30 years. He skimped on sleep and often ate fast foods. He often complained of insomnia and how many pills he had to take for various chronic illnesses.

"You look great to me," I said. "I can hardly believe you have all these problems."

"I don't," he said. "Not any longer."

He explained to me how he got his priorities straight, stopped working such long hours, and started investing in his family. He changed his diet, lost weight, and began sleeping better.

Many people fail to understand the value of sleep. Rather than viewing it as a waste of time, sleep is God's way of allowing the body to restore itself. God ordered his people to rest every seventh day and the land to rest—lie fallow—every seventh year to replenish the necessary nutrients.

Israel ignored his commands and became captives for 70 years, one for every seventh year they had neglected to leave the ground fallow.

We all pay for good health. Either we invest in our physical well-being now, or we pay later with prescription drugs to counteract our *loss* of health. This is the principle of balance. Pay now with exercise, adequate sleep, and healthy food choices or pay later for surgeries and prescriptions. We don't need to remind ourselves about the importance of physical exercise and active lifestyle because we all know that. What we need to do is just do it. Get the plan, create the habit, make it part of your lifestyle.

Adequate rest recharges our bodies. The body heals during sleep. We can learn to use our sleep to get the best out of it. I am not talking about the rest only, but to use sleep to step into the different dimension of creativity. Creative minds revive, even in slumber. I have read that Mozart heard yet-uncomposed symphonies while he slept. Salvador Dali visualized complete paintings. He liked to hold a spoon in one hand as he slept. When his hand relaxed enough for the spoon to clatter against a tray, he sprang up and drew what he'd seen.[28]

Sleep serves as a span connecting the spiritual and physical realms. Use rest to your advantage by pulling creative ideas from the infinite spiritual world, then applying them to your everyday life.

On a recent flight, after finishing up some personal business, I checked my watch to see how much longer I would be airborne. Realizing I had another

> ❝ Sleep serves as a span connecting the spiritual and physical realms. ❞

hour until touchdown, I scanned the other passengers. It seemed everyone was involved in watching a movie, so I decided to check the selections for myself.

One movie caught my attention, *Inception*, directed by Christopher Nolan. The main character (Leonardo DiCaprio) has the ability to invade people's dreams and steal their secrets.

The story line made me think about my own dreams. Sometimes I respond uncharacteristically toward some people and wonder if I have had a negative experience in a dream. Other dreams cause an uneasiness in my spirit, causing me to take time to meditate and restore heart peace.

The plot of *Inception* was for DiCaprio to invade a rich man's son's dreams and cause him to distrust his father's business acumen. That idea grew until he believed he could beat his father's success. The lie, planted by DiCaprio, put him on a path of self-destruction.

Never forget that we have an enemy who works hard to penetrate our thoughts with the intent of stealing, killing, and destroying our destiny (John 10:10). He knows the power of dreams as an important spiritual language. He knows God's creative power has the ability to flow through our dreams and change our lives.

We must retire with the right approach so that during the night our spirit can connect to our future elements. Destiny knowledge and information can download into our spirit (subconscious mind) during the sleep. In turn, the process activates the proper mechanisms which will lead us to fulfill our life's mission.

Try these simple tips at the end of your day to prepare to receive from God during your slumber:

- Analyze the day.

- Bless God, others, and yourself.

- Play peaceful music.

- Ask God to use your sleep time for his purposes.

- Be ready to wake up and write it down.

"The best job is a high-paid hobby." Henry Ford spoke those words. When we choose a career that satisfies us emotionally and mentally, it will seem more like a fun hobby than work.

Moreover, true hobbies also play an important role in the area of rest. While most still require mental thought, such as working puzzles, or physical effort, such as hiking, hobbies switch the brain to a more relaxed, creative mode. They recharge and revitalize the body and brain into higher productivity. Such progress honors our Creator, who made us in his own image.

13- Annie Spratt, Unsplash

PRIORITY #6 – PERSONAL DEVELOPMENT

*Only by paying the price of error can one
know the joy of victory and the pain of defeat.*

—Unknown

An orator in ancient Greece had developed a stutter along with a nervous tic as a child. He was orphaned at 7 years old. By the time he became an adult, his guardians had left him without an inheritance. He decided to find justice through the courts.

At that time, prosecutors were required to represent themselves. The young man tried, but he failed entirely. He became determined to overcome his disabilities. First, he hung a sword by his side, so that every time his shoulders twitched, it poked him. After overcoming that, he walked along the seashore. He strengthened his voice to carry over the sound of the waves. Next, he filled his mouth with pebbles to learn how to enunciate clearly. He returned to court, won his case, and invested some of his inheritance for lessons from a renowned teacher. His persistence altered his future, and he became a famous orator of his time. Imagine what *you* can do with God, your loving father who greatly desires your fulfillment!

Every ship leaves port with a *specific* destination point. We are all sailing on the ocean of life. Do you have a destination? Where are you going? A life without goals is as a ship without a rudder. Like the orator, set the goal and keep it in your sights at all times.

The Apostle Paul compared life to a relay race. He allowed no distractions to keep him from the goal, not even self-preservation. Why? So he could "... finish the race with joy, and the ministry which I received from the Lord Jesus" (Acts 20:24 NKJV). Paul is talking about *focus.*

An archery instructor hung a target on a tree and asked his students, "What do you see?

"I see a tree and a target on it."

Another replied, "I see the trunk of a tree, leaves, the sun, and birds flying in the sky."

All the students responded in a similar manner.

Finally, the master turned to his best student. "What do you see?" he asked.

"Only the target."

The master smiled and turned to the other students. "This is a person with focus. He sees the target, the goal, and nothing else."

Personal development requires a *life plan*. First, think about who you want to be in the future. What do you want to achieve in life? Write it down. Meditate on it. Imagine yourself already achieving that picture.

Next, create a yearly plan.

This involves both long-term and short-term goals. Napoleon Hill called a dream a goal with a deadline. Your dream needs to be specific with a deadline. Take the time to write down goals in each of the six areas described in this chapter. A concrete deadline will increase performance and productivity by 10–25%. This amounts to an extra month of productivity for every working year.

Next, write down a three-month plan.

Statistics tell us that 88% of people who make a New Year's resolution fail during the first three months. Long-term goals are difficult to attain on their own. Achieving them is far more possible when one sets short-range goals first. Focusing on three months is far easier for most people than trying to concentrate on a full year.

This makes for SMART goal setting. The first-known use of the acronym, by George T. Doran, occurred in the November 1981 issue of *Management Review*.

S– Specific. What, who, where, and why I want to accomplish.

M– Measurable. How will I know when my goal is accomplished?

A– Achievable. Make sure the goal is not out of reach.

R– Relevant. Does this goal fit with your long-term plan?

T– Timely. Your goal needs to have a deadline and time limit.

Convert your dreams into SMART goals. You are not giving up on your big goals. Rather, you are creating a plan to achieve

> " Destiny is a long-distance race where commitment and sacrifice are key. "

them with small and smart steps, which are easier to measure and accomplish.

Next, break down your goals into weekly and daily plans. It's easier to plan and work about three months at a time. Now, break that down into weekly goals—easier yet. Move on to a daily plan, with a one-hour scheduler.

Make your list and allow a realistic time to accomplish each activity. What gets planned gets done. Once your day is planned out, make it happen. Plan fun time with your family. Don't get so caught up in what you hope to accomplish in the future that you forget about today.

In the book *Great by Choice*, Jim Collins writes about two expeditions to the South Pole in 1911. Amundsen led one team and Scott the other. Both traveled an equal distance under severe weather conditions. Scott decided to take his team as far as possible in the more favorable weather while resting up on the bad days to save energy.

Amundsen's plan was to stick to walking 20 miles per day regardless of weather. On good days his team could have moved forward, but he decided to stick with the plan. Which team would you think arrived at the goal fastest?

Amundsen's. He worked the doable plan laid out before the journey began, remained consistent to it, and achieved the best performance.

Journal. Journaling releases creativity, organizes thinking, and keeps you accountable to yourself. It even has the power to heal, emotionally and mentally. Write down ideas. They don't have to make sense to you in that moment. Just keep writing until the ideas stop coming. Treat those inspired moments as the very breath of God to you. Once you have laid out your life plan, focus on it. Do not get sidetracked and do not turn back.

In April 1976, Ron Wayne, along with two other young men, decided to start a new company. Ron created their first logo. He wrote the agreement of partnership and created the first employee manual for their product. However, after a mere 11 days, he concluded that the venture was too risky and decided to cash out his shares immediately. He pulled out of the company and received his portion of $800.

I watched an interview of Wayne on Cable News Network (CNN). Today, he resides in a modest home near Las Vegas. The company he started with Steve Jobs and Steve Wozniak was called Apple Computer. The goal of the company was to take good products and perfect them. This pushed them to the front of all the competition, making them hugely successful. Had Wayne stayed with the new company, his portion of 10% would have been *22 billion USD.*[29]

Someone once said, "Good is an enemy of the *best.*" Mr. Wayne felt it *good* for him to leave while the company could guarantee him a profit. In doing so, he missed out on the *best*, which would have made him wealthy.

Don't be afraid to reach for God's best. Best is seldom easy, but it is intensely gratifying.

Learning to set goals starts with the first step. The mountain climber starts at the bottom of the peak. The runner begins at the starting blocks. Nobody achieves the goal without the start. Each of us must start before we can finish.

Where each one of us is today is a result of our yesterday. Today's surgeon studied for years to get where he or she is. On the other hand, the inmate in the state penitentiary is in lockup for the choices he made in his past. Our thoughts became the actions that brought us to our current place in life.

Steve Jobs told people that he looked in the mirror every morning and asked himself, "If today were the last day of my life, would I do what I had planned for today?" If he said no too many days in a row, he knew he needed to make a change.

Successful living requires endurance. Destiny is a long-distance race where commitment and sacrifice are key. Set your priorities in order, determine what changes you need to make, as Steve Jobs did, and remain focused on the end goal.

QUESTIONS FOR REFLECTION:

1. What is your purpose in life?

2. Can you see main priorities operating correctly in your life?

3. Create an exact and real life plan or plan of action.

4. Set achievable goals. Be sure to include your spouse as you write down your plans.

Step 6

HABITS

Environment becomes Thoughts — Thoughts ·-→ Emotions — Emotions ·-→ Words
Words ·-→ Actions — Actions ·-→ **HABITS** — Habits ·-→ Character
Character becomes your
DESTINY

My habits interfere with my life;
I've wanted to get rid of them for quite some time.
—CWT, song lyrics

What are habits? Most professionals define habit as a behavioral pattern that, after a period of time, is performed automatically. Many habits are ingrained so deeply in a person as to appear innate. However, in reality, all of them have been acquired during the course of one's life.

Repetition of action, the subject of Chapter 5, determines the habits we form. Those habits form our character, which consequently alters our destiny.

THE IMPORTANCE OF HABIT

Some people would rather let go of great goals
than petty habits.
—Alexander Kumor

Based on general statistics, we know that 90 percent of one's life consists of formed habits. Sayings such as *He's a creature of habit* and *Habit is second nature* express in simple language the truth of how habits make or destroy our lives. Habits shape our behavior, affect our outlook on life, and determine the choices we make.

Habit simplifies everyday life. Once we have learned how to tie our shoes, the task is done automatically, requiring mere minutes to accomplish. As we mature, we struggle to learn to balance a bike, take a few falls, and then enjoy our new bicycle riding habit without a second thought.

Every person is born with and develops needs over their lifetime. The formation of habit eases the growth process. For example, defensive driving is a learned habit that increases the level of safety each time one sits behind the wheel. A good diet coupled with adequate rest meets one's physiological needs. The habits of drinking water and exercise meet those needs. Good study habits help a person achieve knowledge. All these and more assist a person to succeed in life.

Habit also affects community. In my travels, I have had the honor of meeting devout, enthusiastic believers in some countries who, unfortunately, care little for their environment. While their hearts burn hot for our God, their streets are piled with litter. Other countries exhibit total order and tidiness, while the believers there appear to serve God in a perfunctory manner. Both action and failure to act form the habit of the community. Here in the United States, the government enforces that habit of tidiness with litter laws and paid employees to keep our streets, parks, and beaches clean.

Many people assume that once they have committed their lives to Jesus, their old habits will simply vanish away. At times, God does choose to miraculously deliver a person from destructive habits. Other times, he allows us to work to change ourselves. If we had the habit of procrastination before we became a Christian, there is a very good chance that we will continue to procrastinate after our salvation experience. God expects *us* to work on changing our negative habits to positive ones on our journey in becoming more like Jesus.

Many times, as my team ministers to people in our congregation or down in the city, we see great miracles of healing. They dance and jump for joy. For most, the healing remains. For others, the illness returns within a few months.

This concerned me. I asked God why this happens. I felt he told me that healing, healthy lifestyle, and habit are all interconnected. Should God heal a person with a gastric ulcer, yet she continues to eat inflammatory foods, the ulcer will return.

I have seen people like this become disappointed or angry with God. Some walk away from their faith or stop believing in divine healing. They literally turn their backs on living the abundant life because of their own failure to control their behavior through forming constructive habits.

Paul called such believers spiritual children of the faith (Galatians 4:1–3). Like a small son of a millionaire, they have everything God offers at their disposal yet lack the maturity to access it. Sadly, some believers never grow up to fulfill the destiny God intended for them because they refused to change their habits.

Habits hugely affect how we live our daily life, from the way we dress to what we eat, from how we spend our leisure time to the friends we choose. Our environment also affects our habits. If our coworkers, for instance, habitually cheat the boss, it is far easier to do the same rather than give a full day's work for a day's wage as God commands.

Discarding old habits is not enough to live the abundant life. They must be replaced with good ones, because all habits directly affect our circumstances and those around us. Many of our habits could be left over from our former lives before we met Christ. Have we fully changed our environment, where we go, and with whom we choose to associate? This was discussed in our discussion of the importance of environment. We cannot overstress how much our friends, family, and workplace affect us. Changing our spiritual atmosphere starts with the formation of new and wholesome habits.

> **❝** Cultivating positive habits takes time and hard work while bad ones tend to require no effort at all, until we wish change them. **❞**

THE FORMATION OF HABIT

Nothing so needs reforming as
other people's habits.
—Mark Twain

Every baby is born habit free. Their first habits are formed either by training of family members or from observing and imitating them. The child who observes patience and kindness will often incorporate those habits into his own life. The one subjected to criticism and cruelty will often grow up to display the same.

Habits happen without our direction if we are not careful. We can fall into bad habits, such as retiring too late or eating junk food, or we may cultivate good habits that require time, patience, and determination.

Science has proven that habits develop from repeating certain actions. Take swimming, for example. Each style requires certain movements in specific order. In freestyle—the most common—the arms rotate over the head one at a time as the feet kick up and down. The breaststroke requires movements where the arms stay underwater at all times and the legs are drawn close to the body before kicking out. The exact repetition of the swim strokes insure success or failure in propelling the body forward in the water; this developed, conditionally reflex reaction is known in science as dynamic stereotype. Once the swimmer has mastered each style, it settles into the cerebral cortex of the brain. The moment the Olympic swimmer dives into the water, he knows exactly how to move his body because the habit has settled deep into his subconscious mind. The same holds true for learning how to ride a bicycle, drive a car, or build a house.

Cultivating positive habits takes time and hard work while bad ones tend to require no effort at all—until we wish change them. Both good and bad habits become so ingrained in us as to no longer require conscious thought. While many dream of success in life, only the persistent determination to develop sound habits will ensure it.

Every newly formed habit influences our future, which guarantees new results. We cannot intentionally develop a new habit without first clearly defining what we want to achieve by it. After pinpointing the desired objective, we can set about forming the new habit, which after a matter of time, becomes an integral part of our personality.

14- Anete Lusina, Unsplash

90 DAYS TO THE NEW YOU

The first and greatest victory is to conquer yourself;
to be conquered by yourself is of all things most shameful and vile.
—Plato

G. Alan Marlatt, professor of psychology at the University of Washington, stated that it takes up to 90 days to develop a new skill. Once you have started the process of establishing a strong habit, only persistence will bring you to the desired results. The hard work of developing such habits pays off with higher productivity. It improves your spiritual and physical health.

Shortcuts never work in this process. It takes much education to become a professional and long periods of repetitious practice to become a skilled craftsman. It requires years of learning for both.

As it requires months for fruit to develop from germination to maturity, so the Fruit of the Spirit (Galatians 5:22–23) also manifests itself over time. Patience, kindness, self-control, etc., germinate in the soul. It takes time for them to ripen in our lives. Again, there are no shortcuts to success, only persistence and determination.

To successfully change bad habits for good, one must be willing to become a *disciple*. As an older believer, you may think discipleship is only for younger believers. This is not so. Nobody is ever too old to change their mindset by becoming a true disciple. For many, this may seem scary, even painful. The result, however, is always worth the process.

Change *is* painful, yet entirely necessary. Every productive habit formed causes loss. Loss of wasted time. Loss of non-Christ-edifying pastimes or friends. Paul used strong language when he admonished the

Galatian believers to "crucify the flesh" (Galatians 5:24). However, that is exactly what must transpire for us to achieve destiny.

Sometimes it is not only negative habits that need to go but also those good habits that hinder us from achieving the *best*. We are quite hesitant to give up anything with which we feel comfortable. A runner may dislike using a new pair of shoes because the old ones fit his feet so well. However, those old shoes have lost their real value in that they can no longer provide the wearer with the support he needs to achieve optimum performance. The temporary discomfort of breaking in new shoes is worth the end result of victory.

> **❝** Sometimes it is not only negative habits that need to go, but good that hinder us from achieving the best. **❞**

Remember, a person's character is the sum total of all their habits. We have already learned that the only way to develop new habits is to repeat the desired action over and over again. As many have said, *Repetition is the mother of learning.* If we strive long enough, we will surely master it.

The same is true with learning life skills. At first the information may seem overwhelming, yet practice becomes habit that helps us achieve it. In the process we will surely make mistakes. However, each mistake provides invaluable experience that cannot be acquired through merely reading—even the best books. Only those who do nothing never make mistakes. When we apply what we have learned and developed the right habits, those new habits lead us to successful destiny.

In his book, *Habits of Highly Effective Christians*, Ron Meyers reveals how important correct attitude is to one's life. He emphasizes, "It does not matter how you started the race, what's important is what result you achieved."[30] At times you may feel like you are not getting anywhere. Keep pressing on, for the crown is not given at the beginning of the race. It comes at the end. Do not allow temporary setbacks to stop you. Let them become the springboard to achieve the highest results.

The Apostle Paul encouraged one of his disciples, Timothy, to persevere (1 Timothy 4:16). Consistency is the ability of determined people to achieve due to tenacity. As Sir Winston Churchill so famously stated, "Never, never, never give up."

THE PAIN OF SUCCESS OR FAILURE

There are no shortcuts to any place worth going.
—Beverly Sills, opera singer

If you are reading this, you have or will experience struggle at some point in your life. In such times, you must choose whether to endure the pain of success or the agony of failure. Success requires self-discipline, throwing away pleasant time-wasters and conquering the lazy self who seeks to simply get by.

Victory requires struggle. Nothing worthwhile comes easy. The single mother who desires a better life for her children studies late into the night while they sleep. However, after years of persistence, the moment she holds that degree in her hand, all else fades into nothingness. She rejoices in her success.

Pain of failure comes from never trying or from giving up when faced with hard times. The first, either through laziness or lack of self-control, condemns one to exist, rather than live. Content with discontentment, the person drifts through life like a rudderless ship, going nowhere and achieving nothing.

> **Determine to fight for your destiny by denying what you want to do for what you need to do.**

The second, often fueled by discouragement, shame, or shock, such as job loss or unexpected divorce, can paralyze us to inactivity to the point where we lose sight of God's power to help us achieve his purposes for our lives. The end result is nearly always regret.

On the way to your destiny you will experience intense moments of feeling lost and hopeless along with a big desire to give up too early. We all must be prepared to fight that little voice inside our heads that will tells us to quit and give up. You might experience the agony of self-doubt also. We all may doubt of our abilities, knowledge, and decisions we have already made. All our doubts will create a conflict around us and inside us. If you trust God and are going after those God-given plans, you need to learn how to push through your self-doubts and not allow them to delay or destroy God's plan. You have to believe that you will succeed with God, and you have to trust the Holy Spirit in the process. When the right thoughts combine with the right actions, you can achieve anything!

You might experience the pain of losing some friends on the way to your destiny because the path will narrow, and few people are at the top. Don't be discouraged by other people but work wise and hard quietly and let your success do the talking. To be honest with you, many people don't really like successful people.

Be prepared to deal with the pain of jealousy that will come along with your growing influence. It will not be easy, especially if you want to keep a relationship with some relatives and friends. If you would lose them for some time, don't worry; they may very likely come back to you when you reach your goals and become who you want to become. I have seen a few people who became disconnected for a while. Later, those people who avoided or criticized them feel proud of knowing or being a relative of those successful people. Learn not to get upset with those people on the way to your destiny.

Actions produce habits. Habits produce character. Determine to fight for your destiny by denying what you *want* to do for what you *need* to do.

You may want an extra 30 minutes of sleep, but you need that time to sit in God's presence to feel his heartbeat.

Only God has the power to help us overcome our mental battles of self-doubt, discouragement, or questioning of past decisions. Ask the Holy Spirit to reveal which habits need to change and which to strengthen. Through time spent with God *(environment),* asking for guidance *(thoughts),* moving in his direction *(action),* and accomplishing it through habit, you will soon learn, once again, that you can achieve anything.

Success requires struggle. There is no way around this fact. Sacrifice, pain, failure, and commitment are all part of any real pursuit of a fulfilled life. Wise people recognize suffering as an inevitable fact of life and accept it. Any failure has the ability to help you succeed later. Use the mistakes to your advantage. Never lose hope in God. He desires your success more than even you.

DILIGENCE VS. LAZINESS

By making the use of willpower habitual,
you will no longer be a slave to your weaknesses.
—*Robin Sharma*

Habits wield great power over your life. Many people are dominated by controlling habits that keep them from living a productive, satisfying life. Even as new creations in Christ Jesus, we may fail to understand how to achieve a victorious life. To do this, we must identify our bad habits and declare war on them. The Lord will not do this for you. You must do it on your own, although he is willing to help in the battle.

We live in a culture that encourages self-indulgence. After a hard day at work, the majority of our population relaxes in front of the TV until bedtime. Advertisers study their targets (you, the viewer) with extreme care. They understand the power of suggestion, which often leads to habit, by offering tempting commercials of junk food along with hopeful ones for easy weight loss. Cool liquor ads filled with gorgeous women or handsome men all having a good time mask the real danger of full alcoholism. None of these solve problems. They only worsen them.

A fatal enemy of developing productive habits is laziness. Laziness itself becomes a habit that warps a person's character, stunts their thinking, and influences their conduct. People like this prefer to go with the flow and live life without contributing any effort for change.

Most of us want to read the Bible more, pray more, eat right, and exercise. However, many of us fail, a mere day at a time, because change requires effort. Paul himself struggled over this very issue and wrote, "I have the desire to do what is good, but I cannot carry it out" (Romans 7:18 NIV). We all need God's strength to overcome our weaknesses (2 Corinthians 12:10).

I read a story of a famous writer who realized he could increase his productivity by rising earlier in the mornings. However, he loved to sleep late and did not know how to overcome the habit. So, he asked his servant to wake him up at his specified time.

15- https://www.look.com.ua/download/715/1440x900/

When morning arrived, the obedient servant awakened his master. This angered him and he refused to get up. After waking up very late, as was his habit, he got angry with his servant all over again. He accused the man of failing at his task—to awaken the master—and docked his pay with the threat of more severe punishment if the servant failed again.

The next morning, the servant awakened his master, ignoring his anger and protests. Later, the man gave his servant credit for his own success because the servant helped him break the old habit of laziness and form a new one that increased his writing productivity.

BENEFICIAL AND HARMFUL HABITS

The one who changes his place
but does not change his lifestyle and habits
will never change his destiny.
—*Francisco de Quevedo y Villegas*

We don't dispute the fact that we may have habits that we do not like. Yet, it is so much easier to notice them in others rather than examine ourselves. As God placed Adam in a garden and told him to tend it, so we are to tend the gardens of our own lives. We are to cultivate and nourish beneficial habits while we weed out the harmful ones. Since life is filled with countless habits, which do we tend and which tear out?

Physical health affects our emotional, mental, and spiritual well-being. Wake up early and exercise regularly. Even a short walk gives a boost of energy that affects your outlook for the day.

Doctors maintain that those who eat their meals at the same time every day can avoid many health problems. Because of this habit, internal secretions start preparing for food digestion at a certain time, and food is better assimilated.

The Lord wants to see his church spiritually, mentally, and physically healthy. If you consume a diet of junk food, do not be surprised when your health is affected. God expects you to treat your body with respect and keep it in good condition.

Stay focused at work. Arrive on time, clean and well groomed. You will feel better and be treated with more respect. Be courteous, honest, and consistent in your tasks. A cheerful greeting with a smile can brighten the atmosphere in seconds. Encourage your coworkers, especially your subordinates. Kindness costs nothing, yet affects everything.

Harmful habits are as numerous as the variety of insects. Idleness, rudeness, substance abuse, and greed swarm around us, tempting us to take care of ourselves first, often at the expense of others.

> **Consistent prayer is one of the most potent habits we can develop.**

Another harmful habit is financial irresponsibility. In a culture of easy credit, it is too easy to fall into the trap of instant gratification where you buy whatever you want *now*. I have known people who had to quit going to church and cut all recreational activities to take on a second or third job. Why? To pay off their credit card debt.

Attending a good church with sound, biblical teaching is a good habit that helps to root out the bad ones in our lives. When we gather together in one place, we enjoy fellowship with other disciples of Jesus and have the opportunity to encourage one another in the faith.

We worship our Almighty God together, pray in the power of the Holy Spirit together, and study his Word together. This creates a strong bond of communion and accountability, without which it is impossible to enjoy the abundant life Jesus promised his followers.

Consistent prayer is one of the most potent habits we can develop. Through Christ's example, we learn of his dependence on, yet close relationship with, his Father—now *our* Father. Like Jesus, we need constant interaction with our Father to know his desires, what matters to him, and to follow his path.

Another highly important habit to expand is *faithfulness*. The moment we gave ourselves to God, we revoked the right to turn back to our old lifestyle. God's first commandment is to "Love the Lord your God with *all* your heart, and *all* your soul, and *all* your mind, and *all* your strength" (Mark 12:30; see Deuteronomy 6:4–5). The word *all*, which means 'with abandon, unreservedly' is repeated here four times.

It is impossible to become somewhat Christian or somewhat faithful. You are either faithful or unfaithful. It suggests no compromising with sin, complete dedication to serve God and fulfill His will. It is through such people that God desires to accomplish great things.

The second area that demands faithfulness is with our family. We keep our marriage vows through fidelity, grace, and love. Circumstances do not dictate faithfulness. Honoring God's covenant does.

The third area where we need to exercise faithfulness is in the church. The importance of this was discussed earlier in this chapter. The local church is family. It is where we are to display our love for God as well as love for one another.

IT STARTS WITH THE FIRST STEP

The best thing a person can do for themselves
is to regularly leave their comfort zone.
—*Robin Sharma*

We should not attempt to attack all our bad habits at one time, or the task will overwhelm and discourage us. I suggest dealing with one bad habit a month in order to gradually get free of all of them. Make a list of your current habits that you consider destructive to your personal growth. Deal with them, one at a time, in a consistent manner. Be patient. Give yourself permission to fail sometimes. Failure is only failure if you refuse to start again. Learn from it.

Ask God to help you. Enlist the aid of people you trust to keep you accountable. As you slowly replace a bad habit with good, the taste of success will be sweet to you and give you great encouragement to keep going.

Numbers 11:4–6 tells a powerful story of wrong desires. After witnessing the miracle of redemption from Egypt, the rabble who were traveling with the Israelites began pining for the *food* they had left behind to the point of complaining about God's miraculous provision of manna!

> **Remember, each intelligent person is striving to turn his or her intentions into skills and habits.**
>
> *Bill Newman.*

Old habits become a curse to those who cannot or will not break them. They bring curses, destruction, and misfortune. A born-again Christian follows a new, life-giving way of blessings, fruitfulness, and fulfilled destiny.

Apostle James writes in his epistle, "But one who looks intently at the perfect law, the law of liberty, and abides by it, not having become a forgetful hearer but an effectual doer, this man will be blessed in what he does." (James 1:25 NASB). What does he mean?

Blessed suggests the highest level of God's favor, which brings with it joy and spiritual growth. This is what God promises when we make the decision to abide in God's perfect law—the law of liberty.

Bill Newman, author of *Soaring with Eagles*, wrote, "Remember, each intelligent person is striving to turn his or her intentions into skills and habits." No matter where you are in life right now, to ensure you reach your destiny, you must develop good habits and destroy the bad ones.

URGENT VS. IMPORTANT

A good habit is an accumulation of internal capital
that provides enough interest to support you for a lifetime.
—Vlad Mikov

Our culture has developed a lifestyle of constant busyness, which exhausts our nervous systems and causes our bodies to retreat into a self-preservation mode. We have more and more stuff to do. We increase the pace and do not notice how our lives have become a rat-race. We hurry, work, try our best, deliver, fix, load, pay, pray, study, print things out, etc. We do everything in order to complete our to-do lists. As the day goes by, if items are still left in the list, we leave them for tomorrow. Tomorrow comes, and our lists grows even bigger. The moment finally and ultimately comes when we realize that we simply cannot do everything on our list. We lose our motivation, fatigue builds up, and we are ready to give up and at a loss as to what to do. At times, even the job we love becomes a chore. It this case, the long-awaited vacation gives us only brief relief. What can help this situation?

President Dwight D. Eisenhower faced the same dilemma in his life. As a military leader, he faced constant demands on his time. After careful thought, he came to the conclusion that urgent tasks are rarely import-ant, while important tasks are rarely urgent. He prioritized every one of the tasks he faced into one of four categories[31]:

1. Important and urgent

2. Important and not urgent

3. Urgent but not important

4. Not urgent and not important.

The example below shows how to fit the categories into four squares to achieve the following diagram.

	URGENT	NOT URGENT
IMPORTANT	**DO** *Important tasks you need to do now.* • Crises • Deadlines • Problems	**PLAN** *Things you need to schedule to do.* • Relationships • Business long-term strategy • Exercise
NOT IMPORTANT	**DELEGATE** *Tasks someone else can do.* • Some emails / calls • Some meetings • Popular activities	**LIMIT** *Things to limit or not do at all.* • Time wasters • Watching TV / Gossip • Pleasure activities

16- Jamesclear.com

Take time to make your own to-do list. Afterward, plug each item into the appropriate box. Now, your brain can function in a more productive manner as the priorities come into clear focus. Once you've sorted everything on your list, begin working on what is written in the first square. As you can see from President Eisenhower's example, anything that lands in this square has to do with a crisis. Handle the most urgent needs first before moving on to the second square.

If you organize your tasks in this manner, you will discover that Square 1 is seldom long, because it deals only with *urgent* crises, such as deadlines, sudden illness, true emergencies, etc.

As you complete this square, you can now move on to Square 2. Your mind will respond to working at a steady pace over reacting to panic mode. As the mind paces itself, so the body will follow. You will find yourself able to think more clearly and become more productive in your overall life. Every task completed in a timely manner and well executed adds to a sense of accomplishment and fulfillment. Take time to work on your own four squares before moving on the questions below.

QUESTIONS FOR REFLECTION:

1. What habits are you planning to develop this year?

2. Who is going to be your accountability partner?

3. Set aside some daily quiet time to relax and rejuvenate.

Step 7

CHARACTER

> Environment becomes Thoughts — Thoughts ⇢ Emotions — Emotions ⇢ Words
> Words ⇢ Actions — Actions ⇢ Habits — Habits ⇢ **CHARACTER**
> Character becomes your
> DESTINY

Character is like a tree and reputation like a shadow.
The shadow is what we think of it; the tree is the real thing.
—Abraham Lincoln

The next step on our journey toward destiny covers *character*. In Greek, character means *trait*, *sign*, *imprint*, or *image*. Character is the product of one's thoughts, words, actions, and habits. It is the sum total of the qualities in one's deepest soul that manifests in real life situations.

Character is multi-faceted, like a cut diamond. Whether driven by anger or patience, kindness or selfishness, it is the force that determines our success or failure in life. The formation of character starts in babyhood.

I have often asked parents what character traits they want to develop in their young children. Immediately most name off kindness, courage, wisdom, etc. Next, I ask them, "How are you cultivating these qualities?" Many have no idea *how* to develop character. Someone once said, "Stop schooling your children, they will turn out like you, anyway. School yourself."

What we read and watch impacts our character more than many of us realize. Constant reading or viewing of adultery, violence, alcohol abuse, etc. drops deep into our subconscious until we are desensitized to the moral wrong in all. Without conscious thought, we can easily pick up the words and traits of our favorite protagonist, which impacts our emotions, will, morals, and intellect.

❝ Whatever we view, watch, and play affects us. The images sink into our subconscious and change us. ❞

David understood this principle and warned himself to set no worthless thing before his eyes, so it could not fasten a grip on him (Psalm 101:3 NASB). Jesus echoed the same. "When your eye is clear, your whole body also is full of light; but when it is bad, your body also is full of darkness" (Luke 11:34 NASB). In other words, the body itself responds to everything we view through TV or movies or our reading habits.

The young child first develops his character from imitating the adults in his small world. Later, he will model his behavior on that of other adults and his peers. This is where environment, covered in Chapter 1, alters the maturing child's character.

As he matures and parents allow him to make his own choices, a steady diet of violence through movies or video games will desensitize him to the reality of true violence and cause him to act with violence himself. Today, as school shootings increase, some are eager to blame guns, whereas the real problem lies within the shooter's soul. Follow his character. How did he spend his leisure time?

Graphic, violent video games are not *games*. They twist and damage the soul.

Whatever we view affects us. TV, movies, games—the images sink into our subconscious and change us. As believers, we are called to be transformed into the same image as our Lord, Jesus Christ. "And we all, who with unveiled faces contemplate the Lord's glory, are being transformed into his image with ever-increasing glory, which comes from the Lord, who is the Spirit" (2 Corinthians 3:18 NIV). This is why Paul urged the believers to focus their spiritual eyes on Jesus. Gazing on his glory transfers to our own spirits, which transforms us from observing him to imitating the model of our Lord's behavior until it becomes innate.

Character forms and changes throughout each person's life. God-fearing people are willing to examine their own character to see what needs to be changed, then set about through the habit process to do so. They are also unafraid to ask God to search out their hearts as well, knowing any light he sheds on character flaws is to their eternal benefit.

BE AN OVERCOMER

You will truly know a person's character
when he becomes your boss.
—Unknown

Many people today tend to drift through life simply living with what is familiar to them, avoiding challenges that would stretch them and force them to grow. Our society is filled with those who refuse to push through difficulties. For this reason, half of American marriages end in divorce, more children are growing up in a single-parent household, and the suicide rate is increasing. Many bemoan such problems, but few seem capable of solving them.

Solving problems takes commitment, determination and willingness to *do what is right.* Taking ownership for problems you have created is doing the right thing. Looking for solutions without seeking an easy way out is the right thing. That takes integrity.

Sometimes we come across situations that we cannot solve on our own. Should they encounter an accident, even my children can see the problem, an accident. But it takes mature people not only to see the problem but to take care of it. Kids might see a car accident, but there is little they can do. It is expected from adults to be able to call the ambulance and police, take care of the people involved, call a tow truck, call an insurance company, and fill out a police report. It is not enough to state there is a problem. You have to always have a solution.

I have a friend, who says, "We remember most people by the problems they have created for us." Be a problem solver, not a problem maker. No matter what the situation, face it, ask God to help you, and take action.

Overcomers always map out several solutions to a complex issue. They remain focused on solving the problem rather than on the problem itself. Persons of integrity are willing to step up and take the initiative to start the solving process without stooping to blame others or circumstances for their own problems. Instead, they take full responsibility and go into action.

The overcomer uses strategy:

- Figures several solutions to any problem

- Stays focused on the solution rather than problem

- Takes the initiative

- Does not blame others for the problem

- Takes responsibility

Every believer has the overcomer spirit inside. "Everyone born of God overcomes the world; and this is the victory that has overcome the world—our faith" (1 John 5:4 NIV). Jesus already triumphed over *every* evil force (Colossians 2:15). He has full authority over *everything*.

Every person born into God's family also has the ability to overcome the difficulties of life. We *can* exhibit self-control because Jesus resides in us, ever ready to help us. Jesus granted us the authority over *all* our life situations, including the power to respond rather than react to adversity.

Victory means different things to different people. When dealing with conflicts that involve others, author Stephen Covey explains the four possible approaches.[32]

He calls the first *win/win*. This solution comes through compromise or a draw. It is mutually beneficial to both parties.

The second, Covey labels *win/lose*. I win, you lose. This attitude ultimately destroys personal

> ❛❛ Overcomers always map out several solutions to a complex issue. They remain focused on solving the problem, rather than on the problem itself. ❜❜

and business relationships because of the person's determination to win at any cost.

Covey calls the third scenario *lose/win*. Here, the person takes on the role of a martyr, allowing themselves to be used because keeping peace is most important to them.

The final approach Covey writes of is *lose/lose*. Both parties suffer loss through inability to work through a situation. This often breeds the desire to retaliate and further complicates the relationship between the two parties involve.[33]

Paul instructed his readers to be as interested in the well-being and desires of others as our own (Philippians 2:4). God never intended us to walk this life solo. He expects his people to love one another, care about one another, and help others achieve their destiny. True leadership isn't how far we advance ourselves, but how far we advance others. People always move toward a leader who increases them and away from anyone who decreases them.

Christ, who had everything he wanted in his Father's presence, laid it all aside to tend to ours. He is our perfect example. As he is, so we should strive to be. (See Philippians 5:2–11)

He triumphed over death so that we can triumph over *self*.

CRISIS MAKES OR BREAKS

Money does not spoil a person, it reveals
their hidden character traits instead.
—Unknown

Some psychologists and sociologists claim that a person's character is formed by a certain age. Others argue that development continues throughout life. Erik Erikson wrote in *Childhood and Society* that although character is formed in childhood, it can and usually does change through the different life stages, especially those times when the individual is faced with difficulties.[34] Vulnerability to these ongoing life situations further molds the character for good or destruction.

The Chinese word for crisis is written in two separate logograms. One means danger, the other opportunity, or turning point. Successful people know how to turn each crisis into opportunity. How we handle difficulties affects how we build character.

CRISIS

A time of danger   A time of opportuunity

17- Conscious Magazine, Consciousdaily, Jan. 26, 2015

I read a story of a young man who longed to become a journalist. In college, one professor told the young man he was wasting his time and money because he lacked the skills to succeed as a journalist.

As the boy sat, pondering the professor's cruel words and wondering what to do with himself, a woman stopped to ask him why he seemed so upset. After he told his story, she promptly transferred the young man to another class and fired the professor. As an administrator, the woman had the power to assist the boy in his dream by providing a different avenue for him.

However, she could not help the young man improve his ability to learn. The young man's friend challenged him to memorize a new word every day. He helped him with pronunciation and correct usage. The two worked together throughout their college years, challenging and building the young man's vocabulary. As a result of these two people helping him, and his own persistence, the young man realized his dream. In time, he became a renowned journalist. There are many stories similar to that one.

> ❝ Successful people know how to turn each crisis into opportunity. ❞

Dream building requires character. It takes persistence and hard work. This is what God is all about. He wants us to build our character to mirror his Son's and in doing so, we also realize our dreams.

Crisis comes with every stage of life. Erik Erikson (1902–1994) identified eight stages of psychosocial stages in every human's life, from birth to death. Each is a crisis of decision described below:[35]

Infancy Crisis Factors

- A child's area of decision-making at this age is quite small and has to do with either trust or mistrust toward people or circumstances.

- The major part belongs to the parents who show love, care, and attention to their child.

- Interaction/Communication. Care by and time with the father are very important at this age, since they facilitate a boy's proper development as a male.

Childhood Crisis Factors

- A child makes a choice. He decides what he can and cannot do on his own. The initiative is his and if the result is negative it brings the feeling of guilt.

- A distinct ability to manipulate and dictate to the world around them their desires appears.

- If a child does not learn boundaries in their early years, it will be difficult to change their character or impose limitations on them when grown up.

- Frequent punishment as a child can lead to festering feelings of guilt, shame, and insecurity.

Crisis Factors during School Years

- During this period, an individual has to make a choice of what to achieve and what to base his or her aspirations on. Usually, past history, experiences, and values come into play here.

- If a child starts to measure self against others, the inferiority complex develops.

- Such comparison results in rivalry. Failures and bad grades are things that influence the way a person views themselves and others.

- If a child does not receive help or a proper motivation for success from those around, if they did not help develop a child's individual abilities, then the child might be doomed to a "low flight."

Adolescence Crisis Factors

- At this age, a person has to make the most crucial decisions that will determine the course of their lives. Young people begin to ponder difficult questions: What do I live here for? Who am I? What is my place in life, in church?

- The future looking obscure and uncertain might lead a person to a depression, which will not allow them to make sensible and wise decisions.

- The desire for independence might lead to rebellion.

Young Adulthood Crisis Factors

- A young adult faces the second most important matter of life, choosing a spouse.

- At this age, a person should have settled their education and career matters, found the right job.

- Self-acceptance is an integral part of personal growth and identity formation.

Adulthood Crisis Factors

- The adult also faces serious decisions: to continue living a productive life or to start slowing down to a stop.

- The decisions made at this age impact future generations.

- An individual realizes their ability to give and pass down what they have acquired: abilities, expertise, skills, and assets (possessions).

- An individual who does not have a vision for the future is not getting anywhere, which results in apathy and disappointment.

Crisis Factors in Advanced Age

- This is the time when a person looks behind and evaluates everything they have achieved.

- A person with a properly formed personality is able to accept the fruit of his life without regret.

- Dissatisfaction with the way one has lived their life, being unable to accept the fruit of one's life, leads to disappointment and self-pity.

- A person should be able to take responsibility for who they have become.

Crisis builds character. Character, in turn, requires the subjugation of our selfish desires. As believers, we know that God made us into a new creation through our salvation experience. However, the old natural desires remain for us to subdue. Only through absolute dependence on God will our new nature prevail. This battle continues until our last moments on earth. God will not remove our bad traits because he wants us to gain victory over them.

Although character building remains intangible, in that it lies in our deepest spirit, the results are quite visible in how we conduct our everyday lives. The person who spends quality time in God's presence manifests God's presence to others. Hence, building one's spirit is paramount to success.

God saved us to be like Jesus. The only way we can accomplish this is to honestly face our weaknesses and set a plan in motion to overcome them. Developing new habits to subdue the undesirable traits contributes to the building of character—and to reaching God's goal.

I'm sorry, I can't change. This is who I am. Some folks fall back on this trite excuse to avoid dealing with character flaws. In doing so, they ignore God's transforming power. Several German psychologists maintain that all individuals fall in one of four main categories of character traits and are generally a mixture of two with one being dominant.

These categories are sanguine (dominant), choleric (influential), phlegmatic (steady), and melancholic (conscientious). It is worthwhile to take a personality test to discover your own strengths and weaknesses. That would give you more understanding into your basic character and why you do the things you do and why you react how you do.

Understanding the various personalities also helps us understand how we all have strengths and weaknesses inherent in our natural selves. The caring person can also be chronically tardy. The diligent worker can also be self-serving and cruel. We need God to help us expand our natural strengths and bring into submission our intrinsic weaknesses.

Paul called on his readers to imitate him as *he* imitated Christ (1 Corinthians 11:1). Jesus is the ultimate example of a character formed to honor his Father in heaven. He modeled humility, gentleness, mercy, and a myriad of other positive traits.

BUILDING CHRIST-LIKE CHARACTER

The train fights for speed,
Airplane—for height.
A smart man loves for character,
While stupid—for beauty.
—Unknown

I once asked Bible college students to write an essay on the character of Christ. What a shock to discover every one of them wrote only on his redemptive love that took him to the cross for the sake of all mankind. None of the papers showed any *personal* knowledge of Jesus or the fact that they have experienced his nature through fellowship with Him.

Let us look at the many attributes of Christ which should also manifest in our own lives.

LOVE

Hal David's "What the World Needs Now Is Love," sung by Dionne Warwick, sums up humanity's craving. The majority of poems, songs, and literature bemoan the lack of love. Humans long for it, pursue it, dream of it. We yearn to find that one true love to give us ultimate happiness.

Human love, at best, is still flawed, in that we generally choose to love those who will love us in return. God's love, however, is the supreme love, *agape* love. That is, his love is unconditional to all. Unconditional love freely forgives those who harm us, just as Jesus forgave his executioners as they crucified him. He never loves us based on our own virtues or performance. He loves because love is the essence of his being. God loves because he *is* love (1 John 4:8).

We reflect God's nature of love only to the extent of the depth of our connection with him. As God loves without condition, so he requires the same from his children. We cannot fully comprehend why God loves his imperfect human creation with abandon, nor does he expects us to. He simply bids us to take on the character of Christ and love all as he does.

It is humanly impossible to accomplish this in our own strength. We cannot love the unlovable without God's love in us. Only by dying to our sinful nature, dwelling in the presence of God, and appealing to the power of the Holy Spirit residing in us can we love as he loves.

> We reflect God's nature of love only to the extent of the depth of our connection with Him.

FAITH

The next important quality of our Christian character is faith. The word faith, *pistis* in Greek, means faithfulness. Faithfulness is the consistent adherence to Christian principles. Faithfulness is walking out God's Word. Our uncompromising faithfulness to God keeps us in firm relationship to others and on the firm path toward God's plan for our lives.

Without faith, it's impossible to please God (Hebrews 11:6), so our walk with the Lord is dependent on it. Faith is what brings the things God has provided for us from the spiritual realm into the physical realm (Hebrews 11:1). Our faith is the victory that enables us to overcome the world (1 John 5:4). Everything the Lord does for us is accessed through faith. Faith maintains a firm trust in God, no matter what our outward circumstances are. It produces a calm confidence in him and his guidance. Faith requires a willful choice to do what is right in the sight of God. Only unwavering devotion to our Lord provides the inner strength to trust him, no matter what crosses our path in life. We do not obey him out of fear but, rather, love—love of his being, his glory, and his attributes.

Faith is a great power given to us by God. Faith originates with God, and those who have real faith have his faith. By faith we operate in the supernatural, war against the forces of evil, and obtain victory over our base selves. Jesus promised that everything is possible for the one who believes (Mark 9:23).

Just as Jesus was hindered from performing miracles where unbelief ruled (Mark 6:4–6), so we cannot exercise his power in our lives if our hearts are tainted with the same unbelief. Jesus promised his follow-ers the power to move mountains so long as they placed their trust in the omniscient God (Mark 11:22–24). A.T. Robertson was known as the "granddaddy" of all Greek grammarians when he was alive. His book *A Grammar of the Greek New Testament in Light of Historical Research* is considered one of the most advanced Greek grammars. While Robertson agrees with the "faith in God" translation, he emphasizes that *in* doesn't mean *in* as we English speakers think of it. He marks out that the geni-tive inculcates a genus, or kind, and therefore, holds that Jesus's phrase involves the "God kind" of faith.

We cannot move our mountains through faith *in* God, but rather the faith *of* God. Faith in God can produce self-assurance. This does have the power to propel us to reachable goals and acquire success. Howev-er, when examined closely, this is more faith in one's own abilities than true faith. Do not confuse your God-given talents with faith. Moving in the faith *of* God requires total dependence on him and *his* power. God's faith is supernatural, aggressive, and victorious.

When we reach out to God in faith, he in turn touches us. In that touch, he passes to us *his* Spirit, *his* power, and *his* faith. This impartation tran-spires through lingering in his presence; studying his Word, Jesus; and communing with him through prayer and worship.

Each touch leaves the imprint of Christ on us. This happens in our alone time with God but also in a corporate setting. Many have experi-enced the awe and wonder of attending a gathering where the glory of

God invaded the room with such power, those present sank under the weight of it.

I pray now to you, great God of the universe. You are God and you alone. You created all things by *your* faith. May this faith fill the hearts of every reader. May you, Almighty God, in this moment implant your faith in each one. From this day forward, manifest yourself greatly in each life. In the name of Jesus Christ. Amen!

18- Daeun Kim, Unsplash

HUMILITY

Humility stems from our faithfulness to God. Humility recognizes our total dependence on him. The more we rely on God, the more we realize our shortcomings and imperfections before him. Rather than caving in to despair, we rejoice in our own weakness and seek God's perfect strength.

SINCERITY

Sincerity drives us to build open and trust-based relationships with both God and people. Sincerity requires purity in one's heart and conscience. It cannot manifest in a tangle of lies or contradictions among one's beliefs, attitudes, or actions.

Honesty is an important facet of sincerity. It is a driving force for us to remain genuine, avoid hypocrisy, and withstand deceit. Coupled with the love of God, these character traits wield great power for serving people and God. They pave the path for trust in others, providing opportunity to reach a lost soul for Jesus. Both rebuff humanity's natural inclination toward legalism.

Jesus rebuked the religious leaders of his day, not for failing to keep the law—they performed that to perfection—but for not operating in God's essence, which is love. They cared little how much they burdened their fellow man and totally missed the purpose of the Torah, which was to establish a fairness and order for daily living. As they criticized and condemned others, they exalted themselves, totally misrepresenting God to the people.

In the New Testament, Paul admonished the Corinthians for the same thing. No matter how much spiritual gifting we possess, or biblical knowledge or sacrificial living, if we don't operate in God's love, it is for *nothing*.

GENEROSITY

As God is generous, so he calls us to be the same. Generosity is an expression of love for your neighbor and a willingness to serve others. It seeks to share its bounty with those in need. When we bless others with our time, talents, or money, God blesses us. God especially delights in our giving to those who cannot reciprocate.

Generosity breeds kindness. Kindness gives without regard to the recipient's merits. Kindness reveals the heart of God to all humanity. It extends beyond the mere giving of money. It invests in others through time and resources. Such giving extends honor and dignity to those in need. It models God's character and heart.

The cheerful giver receives the joy of the Lord in return. He feels God's pride in a job well done, which spurs him to give even more, to the point of sacrificial giving. It grows into a delightful cycle of giving, sacrificing, and giving more, because the more we bless others, the more God blesses us. Moreover, it is further proof that we can *never* out give God.

CHEERFULNESS

The Spirit-filled believer always exhibits cheerfulness. Discouragement cannot develop in the heart filled with cheerfulness. It breeds a joyful attitude toward life and people.

> **"** The joy of the Lord grants us the supernatural power to overcome in difficult situations. **"**

While each of us experiences trials from time to time, when we call on God, we can remain cheerful *through* the difficulties. The joy of the Lord grants us the supernatural power to overcome. The joy of the Lord is our strength (Nehemiah 8:10).

Cheerfulness is not based on material well-being, business success, or career growth. Our lives extend far beyond the physical realm and all its concerns. Dependence on God keeps all things in perspective, whether experiencing temporary financial setbacks, illness, or a wayward child.

By understanding our true value *in Christ*, we maintain balance through every challenging situation we walk through. Our own cheerful attitude is a powerful testimony to the nonbeliever, who sees nothing but failure, frustration, or defeat though life's circumstances.

Contentment is vital to maintaining a consistent gladness in our spirit. The chronically dissatisfied are thankless and joyless. Such an attitude infects every facet of our lives from minor inconvenience to major struggles. The mature believer has learned the secret of maintaining full confidence in the one who has everything under his control and who accompanies us through every situation in life.

DECISIVENESS

Decisiveness is the ability to make firm, quick decisions. It sizes up a situation, studies every option, and then acts. It anchors our emotions against the angst, hesitation, and doubt. Such an individual refuses to live in a world of doubt, wondering if she made the wrong choice. Should he discover he erred, he refuses to dwell in regret. Rather, he accepts responsibility and recalibrates. With a resolute heart, he moves on.

Decisiveness is imperative in difficult circumstances. It provides the necessary boldness and courage to push through them. It fuels the heart to move through the trial, day by day. It manifests the character of Jesus when he determined to go to Jerusalem to die for us. Nothing stood in his way. Nothing sidetracked him. So are we, as God's sons and daughters, to be the same.

SELF-CONTROL

John Milton once said, "The one who rules his inner being and controls his passions, desires, and fears is greater than a king." How true. In a previous chapter, we read how a young father flew into a rage and killed his own son. Lack of self-control harms us and everyone around us.

In the chapter on *actions*, we discussed goal setting. For some of us, this requires a great deal of self-control to form the necessary *habits* to improve our lives. We may wish for a better job, higher education, or a slimmer body, but without determination to back it up, it will never happen.

Three of the four gospel writers record a meeting between Jesus and an upstanding young man who lived a principled life. He was drawn to the teachings of Jesus and wanted to know how he could obtain the eternal life Jesus talked about. He was challenged to release what he valued most in life, his wealth, However, he lacked the self-control to pursue what his heart wanted—eternal life. His weakness left him physically wealthy but eternally bankrupt. Self-control empowers the person to push past emotional and physical impulses to achieve the ultimate goal.

Loving our enemies and doing good to those who wrong us takes supreme self-control—until we love as Jesus does and see every human as he does. Self-control enables us to pray for those people who harm us and to forgive them, just as Jesus forgives us.

As Peter wrote in his eight steps toward spiritual maturity, "Make every effort to add to your faith goodness; and to goodness, knowledge; and to knowledge, self-control; and to self-control, perseverance; and to perseverance, godliness; and to godliness, mutual affection; and to mutual affection, *love*" (2 Peter 1:5–7 NIV).

Self-control helps us weigh what matters for now against what matters for eternity. It makes the difficult choice of crucifying our natural desires to press on for the ultimate good, partnering with God on earth and dwelling with him in the hereafter.

Self-control also requires perseverance, or persistence. I read an ancient legend about young men who thought they wanted to become Shaolin monks. They all knew a test was required for admittance. One day, many gathered from the surrounding villages and waited at the monastery gates, ready for their test. They waited in the sun all day. Nobody opened the gates to welcome them.

That night, they all shivered in the cold, and by the next morning, some decided to leave. Another day passed. And another. Some days it rained. The boys ran out of the food they had brought with them. Every morning, more returned to their homes. Finally, when only a few boys remained at the gate, a monk came and opened it.

"When will you give us the test to see if we are worthy?" One asked. "When will we know if we're accepted?"

The monk studied each face. "You are all accepted. You have all passed the test. Because you refused to turn back after days of waiting, even through rain and lack of food, we know you are all capable of enduring the rigors of this place. The weak left. You remained."

No matter how old you were when you entered God's kingdom, you entered as an infant. Just as it does for the human infant, character building begins at the moment of your new spiritual birth. Maturing takes time and patience. You must determine in your spirit how you will mature: growing in God's plan for you or living spiritually stunted. God himself allows difficult situations to mold and perfect us. He cares more about our fulfilling his purpose than getting through life in selfish tranquility.

Young parents may lack the wisdom to know how to pull the best traits from their children, but God created us, so he knows exactly what each one of needs to make us more like Jesus. He is a skilled educator and a perfect dad. Adversity is not designed to torment us. He allows it to teach us to trust him, no matter what, and gain victory over it.

Sickness, disease, and oppression do not come from God. Nobody enjoys suffering, yet it is an important element in the process of maturing in Christ. Like an adolescent pining for the freedom of adulthood, we sometimes chafe against the responsibilities that come with it. Some grew up under the notion that once we become believers, we are assured of a worry free, painless life because we now belong in God's family.

This is a serious miscarriage of truth. Jesus taught his disciples to pray for God's kingdom to reign on earth as completely as it does in heaven (Matthew 6:10). We know the enemy robbed Adam of his inheritance and Jesus won it back on the cross. However, the enemy will not simply limp away and concede defeat. We are in a war, and Jesus promised it must be won through force: "The kingdom of heaven suffers violence, and violent men take it by force" (Matthew 11:12 NASB). We are in a battle until the moment we leave the planet.

Hardships drive us either to bitterness or to God's arms. The serious soldier of Christ leans on God through prayer, reading his Word, meditation, and fasting. Troubles mold us into battle-tested veterans, disciplined in every aspect of our beings.

Fasting definitely requires us to display self-control in that we are placing the desire for spiritual truth over physical needs. Yet it is a powerful weapon in our arsenal. Fasting humbles us before God, bowing us to his will with our spirit in full agreement. It forces the body to submit to the higher purposes of the spiritual realm.

Merely abstaining from food, if we fail to couple the discipline with fellowship with God, accomplishes nothing except a growling stomach. Fasting is a means to express devotion to our Lord as our spirits approach him with loving worship, while our physical bodies experience lack. Fasting strengthens our spirit while subduing our carnal desires.

Such discipline is not self-flagellation, or self-punishment. No, it is an expression of our own inadequacies. It displays our desperate need to depend on him for all things. Physical deprivation strengthens spiritual resolve. Fasting sharpens our minds to our own weaknesses so that God can show us strategy to overcome them. The weapon of fasting helps recalibrate us to our full destiny.

SCHOOLED IN ADVERSITY

Character is the most important
condition of beauty.
—*Sophia Loren*

Tests are not torture. Tests assess progress. Students take tests to find out if they are prepared to advance to the next grade. Teens take exams for a driver's license. Tradesmen test to learn the extent of their skills. Professionals test at every level before obtaining a degree.

The Bible records numerous tests. The Israelites failed a major test of faith. As a consequence, they spent forty years wandering around in the desert before finally advancing to their Promised Land. Solomon passed the test of humility when he requested wisdom. Mary passed the test of total submission by offering herself to be the earthly vessel to bring forth the Messiah.

How we respond to God's tests determines our progress toward destiny or our regression into bitterness, discontent, and regret. Trials expose our heart. They show where we have already advanced and where we need to improve.

> **The full story of salvation is God wants to partner with humanity to bring heaven to earth.**

We are far more apt to fail a test when we are alone, weary, or hungry, or when we have just experienced a time of success. We must take care of our physical selves so that our body serves us, not so we serve it. Surprisingly enough, we can be most vulnerable to fail a trial after a huge success that has drawn upon our reserves of physical, emotional, and spiritual energy.

After Elijah called down fire from heaven and exposed the falseness of Baal worship, he panicked and ran from Jezebel. Only through refortifying ourselves through fellowship with God and other believers who encourage us can we pass the test of adversity and advance.

Some people who avoid the rigors of building character may use the excuse that Jesus loves them the way they are, which he demonstrated by dying for them where they are. It is true that Jesus loves us as-is, but he also loves us enough to want us to change. He desires us to live as his son did on earth.

One of the misconceptions embraced by the church is that Jesus died for our sins so we can go to heaven. As true as that is, it is only a fraction of the truth. Jesus did bridge the gap between God and humanity through his death and resurrection. However, the full story of salvation is that God wants to partner with humanity to bring heaven to earth. He desires to saturate the earth with his glory.

To do so, he needs Spirit-filled believers. His goal is "that the body of Christ may be built up until we all reach unity in the faith and in the knowledge of the Son of God and become mature, attaining to the whole measure of the fullness of Christ" (Ephesians 4:12–13 NIV). This is God's ultimate goal for our lives—containing the full character of Jesus *in us*.

God never hands out a map at the moment of our conversion, explaining step by step his plan for our lives. When difficulties arise, we must set our hearts to accept that anything God allows to happen is for our good. Like a sculptor, he chips away at the shapeless block of marble until a beautiful figure emerges. Nobody studies the chips littering the floor. The eye is drawn to the beauty of what has remained, unchipped, untouched. So God, with great patience and one chip at a time, works to draw out our real selves, which he created to display his character and reflect his glory.

QUESTIONS FOR REFLECTION:

1. What would you like to change in your character this year?

2. What crisis factors are you presently going through in your life?

3. What can you learn from these factors?

Step 8

DESTINY

Environment becomes Thoughts — Thoughts --→ Emotions — Emotions --→ Words
Words --→ Actions — Actions --→ Habits — Habits --→ Character
Character becomes your
DESTINY

I read a parable that I would like to share here. In this story, a man asks the Creator if every person's life is predetermined long before their birth and written in the Book of Destinies.

"I grant each person a certain gift upon birth," Creator replied. "You mortals call this gift 'Destiny.'"

"So, does this mean that the Book of Destinies truly exists?"

Creator pulled a book from nothingness and handed it to the man. He opened it to a random page and began reading about his life.

"Then, everything is meaningless," he said, putting the book down. "All fear, joy, hope, and doubt is already determined. I'm nothing more than a puppet, doomed to play out a preset role."

"Keep reading."

He reopened the book and turned several pages. Every thought, emotion, and deed of his life stared back at him from the written pages. He read until he found nothing but blank pages. As he looked, letters appeared from nowhere to form a sentence.

"This book is recording my destiny," he gasped, "as I live it!" From the corner of his eye he saw the letters becoming a sentence, "He said, "The book is recording my destiny."

"Yes," Creator replied. "In this moment, and every moment, you create your destiny."

Fate, destiny, divine meddling—this topic has intrigued humankind since recorded history. Various religions theorize whether fate is sealed before our birth or whether each human has control over one's own future.

My students often pose various questions about destiny.

"Do I have any say in my future?"

"Does God control every aspect of my life, down to my career and who my spouse will be?"

"Can I change my destiny?"

God informed Jeremiah, "Before I formed you in the womb I knew you, before you were born I set you apart; I appointed you a prophet to the nations" (Jeremiah 1:5 NIV). It would appear that Jeremiah had no choice in the matter because God had already predetermined it. Jeremiah had to be a prophet because that is what God wanted.

We may balk at such a statement, resent it, and even consider it cruel. However, in the same book, God avers, "I know the plans I have for you … plans to prosper you and not to harm you, plans to give you hope and a future" (Jeremiah 29:11).

Although, as humans, we may tend to focus on individual destiny, this is not God's ultimate goal. He wishes to bring every personal destiny into his universal plan—the *ekklesia* operating as Christ's body with Christ as the head, ruling both the seen and unseen worlds. God has established his purpose (Isaiah 46:10–11), and he *will* fulfill it.

Before we ponder further, let us take a look at various world philosophies before turning back to God's Word.

The first use of the word *destiny* in human history is attributed to Heraclitus (c. 535 BC – 475 BC), a Greek philosopher, with the quote, "Character is destiny." He argued that life is not subject to the whims of blind fate, but rather one can control destiny through one's own moral character. Socrates (died 399 BC) also believed man capable of overriding fate through his own will.

Both Hinduism and Buddhism teach the concept of karma. The sum of the individual's deeds—good and bad—determine his future existences. Hindus seek to unite to the great soul through many rebirths while Buddhists focus on reaching Nirvana, a state of absolute nothingness.

Zoroastrianism teaches that a person is free to choose good thoughts and deeds while destiny is predetermined by fate. A person can only escape eternal destruction through good deeds.

Ancient Slavs believed that every event in a person's life was fixed by the goddess, Karna, leaving individuals no control over their futures. They also believed that each person's fate hinged on the behavior of one's ancestors.

Taoists maintain that laws of nature regulate nature and all humankind. Followers can only achieve true wisdom by realizing the futility of attempting to change anything in their world. Therefore, they seek to reach the place of Dao, or inactivity in spirit to achieve harmony of life.

Many persons throughout history, no matter the geographical location, feel that fate controls their lives to the point of them being mere puppets to its capricious whim.

Some believers fall into the trap of trusting fate over faith. Some dabble in horoscopes or other means of foretelling the future, rather than trusting in our loving God, the Father who always wants the best for every child.

THE POWER OF SUGGESTION

Victory in defeat, there is none higher.
—*Robert Heinlein*

Many years ago I heard a story in my hometown about a young man who trusted in the horoscope. He read one that warned that all persons with his Zodiac sign would experience pain in their ears the following day.

He remembered the prediction as he awakened the next day. *No pain.* However, he soon felt a dull pain that progressed to real pain as the hours passed. He complained of the discomfort to a friend and showed him the horoscope.

"I was warned this would happen today."

"Look at this," the friend said, pointing to the date at the top of the newspaper. "This is from last month!"

As demonstrated in the above example, the power of suggestion is real, and it is strong enough to affect us at every level—physical,

> **"** Our mind constantly gives a command to either destroy or create our life. **"**

emotional, mental, and spiritual. The young man's *expectation* became his reality.

Dr. Caroline Leaf, a neuroscientist, maintains that 75 to 95 percent of all human diseases are directly related to a person's thought life. Because our mind constantly analyzes information, it reacts to what we feed it. It gives a command to either destroy or create. Therefore, belief in omens and horoscopes creates a *subjective* reality for the person who follows them.

Unfortunately, there is also division in the Christian realm as several major doctrines prevail in an attempt to explain *fate*. One side believes in 100 percent predestination. They argue that God set the course of all humankind before creation. Through his sovereign right, he predetermined who will be saved and who will be lost. Nothing the individual could do will change God's mind. He simply lives out his earthly life according to how God already set it—either to eternal life or eternal damnation.

On the opposite end of the argument are those who maintain that God grants every human individual choice, not a fate already established in eternity. This places responsibility on each human rather than on God alone. They stress that each individual has the right to choose whether to serve the Lord or oneself.

Followers of both doctrines seem to have many Bible passages to back their arguments. Although they seem diametrically opposed, the doctrines share a common thread, as explained by the Apostle Paul.

"For those God foreknew he also predestined to be conformed to the image of his Son, that he might be the firstborn among many brothers and sisters. And those he predestined, he also called; those he called, he also justified; those he justified, he also glorified" (Romans 8:29–30 NIV).

The key word in this passage is *foreknew*. Because God lives outside of time, he already knew those who would receive and those who would reject him *before* their births. He knew who would embrace his plan and purpose. Those are the ones he predestined to join Christ's body and fulfill Christ's purposes on the earth.

19- Evie Shaffer, Unsplash

ANCIENT AND MODERN HEROES OF FAITH

We cannot be considered the masters of our destinies
until we are the masters of our hearts.
—Unknown

We have no control over the when and where of our birth or over our birth family's social and economic status. However, each of us possesses a knowing in our spirits that causes us to reach for, or sidestep, greatness. God offers to partner with us to transform our lives from ordinary to extraordinary. He is still looking for more Joshuas, Davids, Martin Luthers, and Ira Sankeys to shake the world.

Joseph remains an inspiration and favorite hero of the Bible. God told him of his destiny through dreams when Joseph was a young boy. Joseph believed God, even when that destiny seemed an utter impossibility.

His jealous siblings sought to crush his dreams by selling him into slavery. Joseph ended up in a strange country and moved from slavery to imprisonment under false charges. Personal integrity motivated him to give his best at all times and never stop believing God to fulfill the promised destiny.

After many years, God raised him up to be second-in-command of the most powerful nation on earth. Not only did Joseph save Egypt, his wisdom and foresight saved other nations as well. In time, he saved his own family and was reunited with his father.

Joseph could have derailed his magnificent destiny at any time by compromising his integrity, cheating his master, or turning his back on

God. However, he stayed true to the call God placed had on his life and thus reaped huge rewards.

Maria Woodworth Etter (1844–1924) is a more contemporary example of a person who understood her destiny and refused to allow anything or anyone to thwart it. As a teen, she felt God wanted her to preach. This came at a time when it was unthinkable for a woman to do so.

Because of her father's untimely death, Maria put her dream on hold. She helped raise her younger siblings and then married.

One day, in a powerful vision, she felt angels carrying her to a huge field in the west. She saw herself preaching to the corn and the ears falling to the ground at the sound of her words. She knew she had to preach.

Five of her six children died young. Later, she divorced Philo Horace Woodworth for infidelity and remarried. She and Samuel Etter, her second husband, traveled and preached together until his death twelve years later. She continued her schedule of travel and preaching for many years.

Maria Woodworth Etter pioneered the Pentecostal movement long before the Azusa Street revival. Reviled by many yet revered by more, she never lost sight of her destiny. Whole cities experienced revival under her teachings. One woman moved the nation because God had moved her.

Billy Graham (1918–2018) was a world-renowned man of great faith. However, few people know that, as a sixteen-year-old boy, he resented what he considered boring messages despite his birth into a family of strong believers.

He searched for God's truth with a deeply sincere hunger to know more than just what the Bible said. He wanted to experience the constant presence of God. Once he encountered God in this intimate way, he dedicated his entire life to serve him.

Still, he faced serious challenges. Twice he failed to graduate from Bible schools. He was assigned such a small pastorate that sometimes nobody showed up. He refused to quit, sometimes preaching to the nearly empty room with the same fervor as though it were packed out. God honored his faithfulness by dropping into his spirit a new concept for reaching people with the good news of the gospel—crusades. Author Roberts Liardon claims Billy Graham preached to at least 215 million people in over 185 countries—amazing for any one person. Millions others heard his sermons via television, video, cinema, and internet broadcasts. More than 3.2 million people responded to his invitation to devote their lives to God.

Billy Graham preached to troops during the Korean and Vietnam conflicts. Many presidents confided in him. George H.W. Bush named him America's pastor. However, he never lost focus of his true calling—to tell the world the good news of Jesus.

Nick Vujicic, the Australian born without arms or legs, has inspired millions of people all over the globe. He faced many struggles in his childhood, knowing he would never

> The list of heroes in Hebrews 11 is not yet complete. Any one of us could have our names carved into that wall of faith.

be like any other kid he knew. He experienced deep disappointment, sorrow, and loneliness. He questioned the value of his life and sometimes sank into depression.

His parents determined to raise him to be as normal as possible, encouraging him to find solutions to his unique problems rather than avoid them by giving up the struggle. After he developed a close relationship with God, he began understanding his special purpose in life.

In his book, *Life Without Limits: Inspiration for a Ridiculously Good Life*, Vujicic maps out what he refers to as the main ingredients for happiness. He wrote that every person needs to:

- maintain a strong sense of one's meaning in life;

- maintain a strong and unwavering hope;

- keep faith in God and his infinite mercy;

- live in love and self-acceptance;

- keep a right attitude toward life;

- maintain a steadfast spirit;

- be ready for change;

- keep a strong heart;

- always be on the lookout for new opportunities;

- maintain the ability to estimate risks and laugh at life;

- and be willing to serve people.[36]

Today, Vujicic does not consider God cruel for allowing him to be born without arms and legs. No, he realizes that his physical disabilities have given him the unique ability to touch millions of lives. People who would pass him on the street if he were normal, sit and *listen* to what he has to say.

Nick Vujicic embraces his destiny and lives life to the full. God offers the same possibility to everyone who follows him. The list of heroes in Hebrews 11 is not yet complete. Any one of us could have our names carved into that wall of faith.

EMBRACE YOUR NEW IDENTITY

The devil knows who you are,
God knows who you are,
creation knows who you are,
it's only you who don't know who the heck you are.
—Kris Vallotton

What has helped all the heroes of faith throughout history and today? Every one of them found their identity in God. Every person in the long line of humankind possesses a unique, identifying fingerprint. Everyone born of God possesses the same in the spirit realm.

Once I realize my identity is *in* Christ, everything changes. How I approach life, how I tackle difficult situations, how I see myself. *All* changes through this powerful revelation.

It has been proven that different parts of the brain respond to those situations, depending on how the individual thinks. One part activates when a per-

> ❝ What has helped all the heroes of faith throughout history and today? Every one of them found their identity in God. ❞

son listens to their heart while another reacts when listening to the intellectual mind.

When people make decisions based on their old identity (outside of Christ), they activate the part of their brain which works from the survival mode. In the survival mode, the mind works against the heart and closes out its life-giving wisdom and directions. When that individual returns to the truth of God's Word and remembers he is now in Christ, the brain responds with life, hope, and solutions.

We can only find lasting success by developing a healthy identity in our relationship with God. That achievement, in turn, affects every area of our life in a healthy, positive manner.

When we alter our sense of self, every perception changes. That which used to threaten us is now overlooked. That which once made us fearful is now an exciting challenge. In the book *Transforming Stress: The Heartmath Solution for Relieving Worry, Fatigue, and Tension,* Doc Childre and Deborah Rozman, PhD, compare our perceptions to riding a roller coaster. Some people are in the front throwing their hands in the air laughing and screaming for joy. Others huddle in the back, covering their eyes and crying out in terror. They are all on the same ride. What is the difference? Perception.

How we see ourselves moves us from paralyzing panic to enjoying the ride of our lives.

The Apostle Paul prayed for us to embrace "the mystery that has been kept hidden for ages and generations, but is now disclosed to the Lord's people. To them God has chosen to make known among the Gentiles the glorious riches of this mystery, which is Christ in you, the hope of glory" (Colossians 1:26–27 NIV). We all can read this phrase and understand the meaning of these English words, but it doesn't mean that the mystery has been open to us. It's an experience, not just intellectual reasoning on the mystery. It's not enough to understand with our mind, it's supposed to be seized and embraced by our entire being. As we clothe ourselves in *his* identity, we are enabled to live his full and glorious life *in us*.

In Christ. This is the key that unlocks divine destiny. Paul understood its importance so much he wrote *in Christ, in him*, or *in the Lord* at least 160 times. He knew this principle is the only way to achieve the victorious life.

In fact, all of creation waits with eager expectation for the revelation of the sons of God (Romans 8:19). Our understanding of this truth changes every part of us *and* our environment. God has charged us with bringing redemption and his glory to earth.

According to the Bible, we are seated with Christ in heavenly places (Ephesians 2:6). Unfortunately, some Christians are having an identity crisis. They don't know who they are in Christ or where they are seated. Instead of identifying with Christ, they identify with the problems that confront them.

Did you ever notice in the Scriptures that God often changed people's identities? They looked at themselves one way, but God told them who they really were. This is what happened to Gideon, Abram, David, and others. God calls those things that are not as though they were (Romans 4:17). In the natural realm, what God is calling us may not exist. But in his eyes, it does. So we need to talk about ourselves the same way God does.

How can you achieve this new identity? Begin by understanding your life from heaven's perspective (Colossians 3:1–4). Place *all* your confidence in Jesus. Understand that he remains with you through all the mundane tasks of everyday life. He stands by you at work, in recreation, and as you sleep.

Relax! Love God and people. In everything reflect Jesus (Colossians 3:17). Choose to believe what God says about you. Your feelings do not define you. Nor do circumstances or the opinions of others. Neither success nor failure, financial straits nor affluence determine who you are. Only *God* determines your true identity.

In the mirror we can see our physical identity, but how can we see our spiritual identity? The spiritual mirror is our Bible. Use the following verses to establish this truth in your deepest being:

- I am a new creation. 2 Corinthians 5:17

- I am forgiven of my sins. 1 John 1:9

- I am now a child of God. 1 John 3:1, 2

- I am valuable to God. Matthew 6:26

- I am a child of God and a co-heir with Christ. Romans 8:17

- I am more than a conqueror through Christ. Romans 8:37

- I am accepted by Christ. Romans 15:7

- I have the mind of Christ. 1 Corinthians 2:16

- I am washed, justified, and sanctified through Christ. 1 Corinthians 6:11

- I am righteous in Christ. 2 Corinthians 5:21

- I am a saint. Ephesians 1:1

- I am complete in Christ. Colossians 2:10

- I am holy in God's sight, without blemish and free of accusation. Colossians 1:22

- I have been made rich. 2 Corinthians 8:9

- I am of a chosen people, a royal priesthood, a holy nation, a people belonging to God to declare the praises of him who called me out of darkness into his wonderful light. 1 Peter 2:9

- I am born of God, and the evil one (the devil) cannot harm me. 1 John 5:18

10- Joshua Hanks, Unsplash

> **When people make decisions based on their old identity (outside of Christ), they activate the part of their brain which works from the survival mode.**

The moment you embraced Christ, he made you a new person with a new destiny. "If anyone is in Christ, he is a new creation; old things have passed away; behold, all things have become new" (2 Corinthians 5:17 NKJV). You are a brand new person inside, and a new life has begun. You are now identified with Christ and have the power of the Holy Spirit within you. You are God's precious child, whom he created for abundant life. Stand up and be who God says you are!

WHAT ABOUT YOUR FUTURE?

The fortune of the man who sits also sits.
—Philip José Farmer

God is good. He loves his creation. When difficult circumstances arise, He comes alongside each one of us to help us. He longs to see us achieve total victory in everything.

God conceived a perfect destiny for every one of us. However, he did not create us as preprogrammed robots. His desire is to partner with us. As we listen to him, we come into alignment with him and thus fulfill his great plans.

This entire book is dedicated to showing us how to achieve this perfect, predetermined destiny, through the seven areas of necessary development. We already know that no disability, setback, or external force can deprive us of our destiny once we have determined to place ourselves under God's protection, guidance, and power.

The Lord already knows our entire inner essence. Nothing surprises him or takes him off guard. No matter the circumstances of our birth, or developments in life, he always wishes to bring us to our highest potential physically, mentally and spiritually. Nothing nor anyone can stop the plans he has made for each of us, except us.

King Saul is a person who thwarted his own destiny through willful disobedience. He began his reign as Israel's first king under a huge anointing from God. Sadly, he destroyed God's intentions for his life through arrogant impatience by usurping the priest's role and offering a sacrifice on his own. As a result, he lost the throne his descendants should have inherited to David.

> There are no accidents in destiny; a man rather creates than meets his destiny.
> —Abel-François Villemain

David approached his God-given honor in a whole different way. As a worshiper, he enjoyed a deep, intimate relationship with his Creator. He knew God's heart and yearned to be in total alignment with it. Although he stumbled late in his reign, he ran back to God instead of away. He confessed all of his sins, and God restored the intimacy that drove David's life.

Ask yourself: What are the deepest desires of my heart? Do I want to go my way as King Saul did, or do I wish to honor God because he truly is the Father who knows best?

I read a parable about a man who wandered into a storage house in heaven. He saw many boxes with names of people written on them. He asked his angel escort if there was a box with his name on it. If so, what were the contents inside?

The angel replied that each box contained all the blessings God foreordained for all humankind. However, the blessings remained in storage, unused, because those individuals never asked God for them. They had failed to tap into all of the mercy, grace and love God set aside for them.

As Abel-François Villemain once said, "There are no accidents in destiny; a man rather creates than meets his destiny."

QUESTIONS FOR REFLECTION:

1. Where do you think God is leading you, your family?

2. Write down the story of your life starting from the present and working back to your career, education, and childhood.

CONCLUSION

Destiny is no matter of chance. It is a matter of choice.
It is not a thing to be waited for, it is a thing to be achieved.
— William Jennings Bryan

I started this book reminiscing about my brother's funeral. The event made me sit and contemplate my own life choices. I sat in my favorite chair as my family gathered around me to comfort me in my loss.

As this work concludes, I find myself in another comfortable chair, drinking espresso in a lovely hotel in London while my wife and children sleep. After exploring the fabulous sights here, we plan to tour Rome, Venice, Corfu, and more before flying on to our home country.

It is an honor to expose our children to diverse cultures, which results in many lively discussions over humankind's view of God, family, and life. When we return to the United States, we will have countless photos to relive these memories many times.

I give all credit to the goodness of my Lord and God's amazing love which has guided me through these past decades. We have already enjoyed experiencing many lovely places here on earth. We anticipate the future with confidence and joy because we know it is all part of God's destiny for myself and my family.

As this writing concludes, the journey of life continues. When I first began contemplating the steps to destiny, I realized the importance of ***environment***, as the foundation for all the following steps.

> **❝** Partner with God and prepare to experience incomparable joy as he leads you to your own great Destiny. **❞**

The home and heart filled with God's presence frees our soul and spirit to move in confidence and security. A Holy Spirit-infused atmosphere tones and trains our ***thoughts***, which become tools to release our God-given potential through imagination and dreams.

As we guard those thoughts and emotions to flow in God's positivity, we learn to speak only ***words*** that propel our life forward into ***actions*** that develop God-driven priorities on our road to success. God-honoring ***habits*** generate the ***character*** that marks us as those who follow Jesus with all our hearts. That character launches us into our life purpose—the ***destiny*** God planned for every one of us before time began.

Through following these steps, my life has prospered far more than I ever imagined back when I was a young university student. However, my decisions have not affected just me. My wife and children have also benefited. Such a fulfilled life is not only for me. God offers it to everyone who chooses to follow him with all their heart, soul, and spirit. Peter affirmed that God does not favor one person over another (Acts 10:34), but longs to see every human live a meaningful life, complete in him.

The Creator's goal is never to bring anyone to defeat or despair. He wishes to bestow abundant life upon all. He gave Adam the opportunity to reach his full potential by instructing him to take care of Eden (Genesis 1:27–28). His natural and spiritual laws continue to this day. God continues looking for persons who will embrace the destiny he has planted into every human heart. Partner with him and prepare to experience incomparable joy as he leads you to your own great ***Destiny***.

21- Jeshoots.com, Unsplash

SPECIAL GRATITUDE

Special gratitude to everyone who contributed to this book. First, thank you, Yana Roshchyna and Anna Shagin, who translated from the original Russian so that more readers could benefit. I appreciate Arlene Baker, developmental editor, and Libby Gontarz, copyeditor, for their efforts to perfect the book. Rebecca Bishopriggs, thank you for your work in correction, also. Finally, thank you, Vadim Makoed and Taras Omelchenko, my book designers, who have carefully crafted the book's appearance to enhance both its appeal and readability.

BIBLIOGRAPHY

Author's note: In this book I refer to both secular and Christian sources. The fact that I have included quotations from some authors in this book does not mean that I fully share and support those authors' positions and recommend their works for reading. Also, much of my original research was done in the Russian language. Where possible, I have updated those sources with English-language references. I regret that it was not possible to find English sources for all pertinent information.

[1] "The Most Famous Wild Children." *Molomo* (in Russian). January 18, 2014. http://www.molomo.ru/inquiry/wild_child.html.

[2] Serov V. *Encyclopedic Dictionary of Popular Words and Expressions*, 2nd ed. – M.: Lokid-Press, 2005.

[3] "The CHILDWISE Monitor Report 2017. *Cision PR Newswire*. https://www.prnewswire.com/news-releases/the-childwise-monitor-report-2017-300408381.html

[4] "Professor Emma Bond." University of Suffolk. https://www.uos.ac.uk/people/prof-emma-bond

[5] "Daily Media Use Among Children and Teens Up Dramatically From Five Years Ago." *Henry J. Kaiser Family Foundation.* January 20, 2010. https://www.kff.org/disparities-policy/press-release/daily-media-use-among-children-and-teens-up-dramatically-from-five-years-ago/

[6] "Defense Blames Rock Song Attorney Asks To Play Song at Teens' Triple-Murder Trial," *The Spokesman-Review.* Jan. 18, 1996. AP. http://www.spokesman.com/stories/1996/jan/18/defense-blames-rock-song-attorney-asks-to-play/

[7] Dunlop, Aaron. "The Juke–Edwards Story: A Contrast in Family Legacy." *thinkgospel.com.*
https://thinkgospel.wordpress.com/2014/10/28/the-juke-edwards-story-a-contrast-in-family-legacy/
See also: "Christian family." Fullref. (in Russian) http://fullref.ru/job_9f6eeae274b-32c9b86e67a8374737593.html

[8] Seymour Epstein, "How Thinking Affects Health." *Elitarium,* February 20, 2014. (in Russian)
http://www.elitarium.ru/2004/02/11/kak_myshlenie_vlijaet_na_zdorove.html.

[9] "12 Facts about Creative Thinking that Are Not Taught in School," *The World of Science and Technology.* November 10, 2012. (in Russian) http://mirnt.ru/statji/12-faktov-o-tvorcheskom-myshlenii-kotorym-ne-uchat-v-shkole.

[10] "Imagination," *Wikipedia*, April 20, 2014. (in Russian) https://ru.wikipedia.org/wiki/Воображение.

[11] Bruce H. Lipton. *The Biology of Belief,* p15. Hay House, Inc., Publisher, 2011.

[12] James Richards. *The Anatomy of a Miracle*, p82. Newburg, PA: Milestones International Publishers 2008.

[13] Hunt, June, Keys. "Christian resources". Internet resource, (in Russian) http://www.kingdomjc.com/Books/Kluchi/07.htm. July 11, 2014.

[14] Joseph Stowell. "My tongue is my enemy." *Russian Baptist Fellowship,* July 12, 2014. (in Russian) http://russianbaptistfellowship.com.

[15] Mary C. Lamia, PhD, "The Power of Hope, and Recognizing When It's Hopeless: Hope Can Alter How You View Yourself," *Psychology Today.* https://www.psychologytoday.com/us/blog/intense-emotions-and-strong-feelings/201106/the-power-hope-and-recognizing-when-its-hopeless

[16] Arti Patel, "Young Adults Stress: Survey Finds 90% of Young Canadians Are Stressed Out," *The Huffington Post Canada.* https://www.huffingtonpost.ca/2012/11/05/young-adults-stressed_n_2039897.html

[17] Alan Henry, "What Stress Actually Does to You and What You Can Do About It," *Lifehacker.* September 2, 2011. https://lifehacker.com/5836879/what-stress-actually-does-to-you-and-what-you-can-do-about-it

[18] Donna Krupa, "More on the Humor-Health Connection: New Study Finds Anticipating a Laugh Reduces Stress Hormone," *The American Physiological Society."* http://www.the-aps.org/mm/hp/Audiences/Public-Press/Archive/08/10.html

[19] Peter P. Garyaev, "Human DNA Research," online video *YouTube* https://www.youtube.com/watch?v=F7T-zYJmybY. For additional information, see also http://wavegenetics.org/en/

20 "Dr. Masaru Emoto and Water Consciousness," *The Wellness Enterprise.* https://thewellnessenterprise.com/emoto/

21 "Influence of Filthy Language on Health, Consciousness, Human Life," *Scmconf.* http://www.scmconf.ru/Ayat-ot-redaktsii/mat_zdorovje_soznanie.html. August 1, 2014.
This site is no longer accessible. For additional information, in Russian, please see: Valery Sirotkin, "Effects of Mat on Health, Consciousness, Human Life," *KOHT.* https://cont.ws/@id271584181/455928

22 Becky Parry, "Amy Purdy: Paralympic Champion, Meningitis Survivor," *Confederation of Meningitis Organisations,* February 22, 2018. http://www.comomeningitis.org/blog/2018/02/amy-purdy-paralympic-champion,-meningitis-survivor/

23 Bill Bright, "The Miracle of a Brother's Song," *Christianity Today. https://www.christianity.com/devotionals/insights-from-bill-bright/the-miracle-of-a-brother-s-song-jan-12.html*

24 Grazyna Fosar and Franz Bludorf, "Scientist Proves DNA Can be Reprogrammed by Words and Frequencies," Collective Evolution, September 2, 2011. https://www.collective-evolution.com/2011/09/02/scientist-prove-dna-can-be-reprogrammed-by-words-and-frequencies/

25 Many versions of this old Jewish tale exist. One you may enjoy: Shoshannah Brombacher, "A Pillow Full of Feathers," *Chabad.org.* https://www.chabad.org/library/article_cdo/aid/812861/jewish/A-Pillow-Full-of-Feathers.htm

26 "Blessing of the Father," *Father's Blessing Spiritual Center,* August 8, 2014. (in Russian) http://www.imbf.org/interesnye-stati/primery-propovedi.htm.

27 Information and trading platform, MQL5, August 8, 2014. (in Russian) https://www.mql5.com/ru/blogs/post/652059

28 "Time Is Ahead, Sleep Is Back," Rossiyskaya Gazeta - Week No. 3438 (in Russian) http://www.rg.ru/2004/03/26/a21483.html. August 14, 2014.

29 "10% of Ronald Wayne," Christian Information Portal, *Uucyc.ru*, October 2, 2014. (in Russian) http://uucyc.ru/story/960

30 Myers, Ron. *Habits of Highly Effective Christians.* St. Petersburg: Biblical View, 2006.

31 "Eisenhower's Urgent/Important Principle: Using Time Effectively, Not Just Efficiently," *Mind Tools.* https://www.mindtools.com/pages/article/newHTE_91.htm

[32] Covey, Steven, *7 Skills of Highly Effective People*. http://baguzin.ru/wp/?p=2727. October 21, 2014.

[33] Library, web-lit.net. Erickson, Eric. *Childhood and Society*. Internet resource, http://www.web-lit.net/writer/forty06/book/11575/erikson_erik_g/detstvo_i_obschestvo/read October 30, 2014.

[34] Erickson, Eric. *Childhood and Society*. W.W. Norton & Company, Inc., New York. 1950, 1963. http://www.web-lit.net/writer/forty06/book/11575/erikson_erik_g/detstvo_i_obschestvo/ (in Russian)

[35] "Erickson's Stages of Psychosocial Development," *Wikipedia.* https://en.wikipedia.org/wiki/Erikson%27s_stages_of_psychosocial_development

[36] Nick Vujicic. *Life Without Limits: Inspiration for a Ridiculously Good Life*. Water-Brook; 2012. ISBN: 0307589749